SAMPLE THE SECRETS OF SUCCESS FROM SAVVY ENTREPRENEUR— SANDI WILSON

BE THE BOSS

RUNNING A SUCCESSFUL SERVICE BUSINESS

SANDI WILSON

AVON BOOKS · NEW YORK

BE THE BOSS II: RUNNING A SUCCESSFUL SERVICE BUSINESS is an original publication of Avon Books. This work has never before appeared in book form.

AVON BOOKS
A division of
The Hearst Corporation
1350 Avenue of the Americas
New York, New York 10019

Copyright © 1993 by Sandra Lee Wilson
Published by arrangement with the author
Library of Congress Catalog Card Number: 92-90538
ISBN: 0-380-76614-0

First Avon Books Printing: March 1993

AVON TRADEMARK REG. U.S. PAT. OFF. AND IN OTHER COUNTRIES, MARCA REGISTRADA, HECHO EN U.S.A.

Printed in the U.S.A.

RA   10   9   8   7   6   5   4   3   2   1

Acknowledgments

Thanks to everyone who has helped us with our business over the years, and especially these people:

Carolyn Raisig, sweet and lovely, who returned one call and pushed us into orbit.

Paul Raisig, who gave us a chance to prove how hard we could work and introduced us to trade associations.

Betty Lou Cooke, whose trust and unfailing friendship has been a source of strength, and who will look great in purple someday.

Ann-Marie Bartels, powerhouse woman, lover of flowers, fudge and slumber parties, and a great friend.

Rick Dobson (see secret #184).

Larry Jennings, who appreciates the efforts of hardworking, creative people, and who never met a bill he didn't process in five minutes.

Sam Lippman, always with the jokes, always ready to whip out the calendar and book a night for dinner in Georgetown.

Linda Donald, Renaissance woman, true warrior, strong survivor, who steered us forward to computers and skylights.

Glenn Gamber, funny, wise, gentle wordsmith, and a man from whom I can take criticism anytime.

Ken Koepper, Ken-O-Rama, The Kenmeister, cuttin'
copy, The Kenmore, devourer of mastodon claws and
Cokes, editor extraordinaire.

Larry Graham, who knows the importance of laughter
and who is, and always will be, a free man in Paris, un-
fettered and alive.

ONE MORE THING:

This book, the first book, and our business would not
exist without the humor, talent, style, wisdom and common
sense of Kathy Pirk, my best friend and co-business owner.
This one's for you, kid.

Contents

Preface

Please read this part before you buy this book:

The easiest thing I ever did in my life was start our business.

The hardest thing I ever did in my life was run that business.

Here is one of the 28 Great Truths—running a business is not going to be easy. You probably know this already.

What you may not know is that for long stretches of time, you won't have a weekend off, or even a day off. You may eat your four-minute breakfast and three-minute lunch leaning over the sink, trying to balance the front page of the newspaper on the roll of paper towels. You probably won't lose weight because your miserable little dinners will consist of such leftover gourmet combos as sweet potatoes with marshmallows, fried rice, a suspicious slice of pepperoni pizza, and potato skins with cheese, then you'll wolf down a package of chocolate cupcakes for the energy you'll need to work late tonight.

If you're like the rest of us, you won't make a fortune. You'll be lucky to make enough to pay all your vendors and have some left to pay yourself a decent salary. You won't have time to take that vacation, and you may even have to work all holidays the first year or so. If you want to pull this off, you're going to have to be willing to give it all you've got, and more.

But the rewards are beyond your wildest dreams.

If you stick with it, you're going to feel as you have never felt before. Your strengths and weaknesses will be tested. You will find humor in the oddest places. You'll discover that you can handle losing, and how much better it feels to win. Every time the telephone rings with more work, each time you land a new account, it's reaffirmation that someone out there believes in you. Every small success you achieve is because *you* worked for it and earned it. You'll know that you are self-sufficient and capable, and you'll know, possibly for the first time in your life, what it means to be free. These things are truly rewarding.

However, so is great wealth.

While I can't promise you that you'll make pots and pots of money, I can tell you that just about every successful big business started out as a small business.

Since the publication of *Be the Boss* in 1985, many people from across the country and in Canada who are struggling to run all types of small businesses have called or written to me, asked me to come and speak at their meetings or groups, or interviewed me for an article. This has been great fun, for the most part. I've always enjoyed talking with people about their small businesses and hearing about their problems and successes.

Once, I agreed to meet privately with a person who was having some major problems getting a business going. This person had read my book, gotten all fired up, and leaped out on her own with no safety net, no savings, no clients, no nothing. Sort of like what we had done back in early 1980. She told me all about how hard it was to make money and how impossible it was to find accounts.

But the worst part was how it was getting difficult to feed the children. That part really got to me. *You* may choose to go on a long diet, but it's illegal to force kids, pets, and any other life forms that depend on you to live this way.

Well, I'm not sure if it's illegal, but it certainly is not right.

I encouraged this person to do anything short of prostitution (i.e., get a government job), and even that, if necessary, to feed the kids. Within a year or so, we heard that the business was doing much better.

The point here is that I don't want you to think that running a business is going to be easy. It won't be. Some people who are well-meaning, dedicated, and hard-working are not going to be able to keep their heads above water.

But you're thinking that your business will be different. And I'm thinking you're right.

Now I dare you to read this book and see if you've got what it takes to start your own business.

Introduction

Secret #146 Secrets #1 through #145 are in another book.

A funny thing happened on the way to my career goal of being a successful novelist and Kathy Pirk's dream of becoming a famous illustrator. We sort of fell into running our own small business and managed to make quite a success of it. There's no Rolls Royce out in the garage, no private jet, or villa in France, but we're doing okay.

Be the Boss: Start and Run Your Own Service Business, my first book, covers much of what we learned in the early years of our business. It's a basic guide for people who want to make the leap into their own business, but don't know where to start. A lot of people (well, like 29 or so) have told me that reading *Be the Boss* was like getting a pep talk, which is wonderful for an author to hear.

It was published in the mid-1980s when most U.S. banks were stable and profitable, and people actually opened accounts at savings & loans, and we were all knee-deep in credit card statements. Back in those heady days, I believed that it was the right time for anyone to start a business, no matter what your age, sex, handicap, race, creed, religion, or bank account figures.

Fool that I am, I still believe that anyone can do anything if you really put your mind to it, and that the time is still right. In fact, it may be more right than ever. It doesn't matter if you're nine or 99, if you look like Lou Grant or Lee Grant, if you are any color in the rainbow. What matters is whether you want to do it enough.

If you have not read *Be the Boss,* then you don't know how different my approach is from all those boring business books out there. What I tried to do with *Be the Boss* was two things:

1. Get across to you that it's all common sense—there is no extraordinary trait or gift that other people have that has somehow eluded you. It's simply hard work, persistence, and of course the ability to not mind that there is a telephone growing out of your ear.

2. Make you laugh, show you that there are lots of funny parts about running a business. Why act as though you just finished making all your own funeral arrangements, for crying out loud.

Make that three things:

3. Encourage you to not use a lot of silly words such as "capitalization" and "negative amortization," when "money" and "loss" will do just fine. Nobody talks like this except corporate accountants and lawyers, and they only talk to each other in that peculiar, humorless language that consists either of words with a dozen syllables or acronyms that they turn into verbs.

If you have read *Be the Boss,* you know all the secrets you need to know about starting from scratch, with absolutely nothing except determination, a little bit of luck, and a stash of Fifth Avenue candy bars. Some of the points I covered in that book include:

1. If you want to do it, don't let anyone talk you out of it by saying that your job is just too good to walk away from, or that you're safe where you are, why take a risk. Nothing in corporate America is safe anymore. Anyone can get fired or laid off; it's happened to millions of us.

2. When you leave a regular job, you must do one of these three things immediately: (a) never get sick or hurt, not once in your life; (b) transfer your employer health insurance to a private policy and have the bills come to your home; or (c) find a new insurance com-

pany to cover you, starting immediately. In fact, try to do the first thing no matter what you do about your health coverage.

3. If you decide to go into business with a partner, there are a few minor things you should consider, such as who does what, how you work together, how you work apart, staking out your turf. Your brand new baby business will need a name, just like any other brand new baby, and you'll have to have business cards printed, decide where you want to work (I push home-based businesses because I believe that this is really where most of us want to work, plus think of all the petroleum you'll never have to buy), and figure out how to start acquiring new accounts. There's a free list of new accounts right in your home. It's called the phone book.

4. The main reason most of us start our own business is to make money. This is something about which you cannot be squeamish, cute, or clever. (Flexible is okay, however.) You have to make sure your clients understand what they're going to have to spend in order to get your incomparable service and finished product. This is why we do estimates and get them signed by the client. Everyone hates bad surprises, so you must revise these critical pieces of paper as necessary (such as when the client makes major changes) and keep getting them signed, and then you'll have that paper trail in case you ever have to take the jerk to court.

You may as well face it—the check is never in the mail. You're going to have to combine the charm of a kitten with the aggressiveness of a pit bull to collect all the money that is owed to you. Obtain lines of credit and sources of cash, because you still have to pay all of your bills. Doing this in the lean times can be a lot of fun. Not.

5. Your image is invaluable. Don't ever tell a client that things are not going well, or that you're having trou-

ble making ends meet. What client wants to hear that his/her star vendor isn't doing so hot? Plus they'll start to wonder if you're paying other clients' bills with their money. If your business is experiencing a minor slump, take your best clients to lunch. If you're really in trouble, take the client to dinner, with good wine. Do this in your best times, too.

6. Nothing should stop your business from going through the roof. Success is an attitude, and you can create it with your vision, sense of optimism, and inner strength. It doesn't matter if you're a man or a woman, black or white or purple, young or not so young, rolling in money or desperately poor. What does matter is your attitude. Many famous high achievers have fought and kicked their way up from the bottom, in spite of handicaps and against all odds. You can, too.

Your positive attitude and honest approach to everything will make others sit up and take notice. You will acquire a greater amount of confidence the more successful you are, and you will begin to notice that more people are taking you seriously because you are the owner of the business.

7. Identify the people who really run the business world, the true managers, the insiders who tell you what's happening, get your message in front of all the others, cut your checks and get them signed, and do countless other vital deeds to help you as you manage your business. They are the secretaries and administrative assistants.

8. Get the whole story before you quote a price to a client. There's nothing quite so horrible as discovering that the materials to do a job are going to cost $2,000 instead of $200, and guess who gets to tell the client, or pay for it yourself?

9. Being organized will not only save time and money for you, it will also save your complete sanity. File

all receipts. Make lists of what you have to do, what can get bagged, and what you can stick on someone else to do. A constantly ringing telephone is a measure of success, as well as the greatest thief in the universe, so get someone else to answer your phone, if possible; return only the phone calls that you absolutely have to return, and don't bother with the others.

10. As your company grows, you may need outside help. Hiring good freelancers or consultants is a lot like winning the lottery. If you're extremely lucky, you'll find someone who cares about your business almost as much as you do. This will most likely be your mother or another close relative who changed your diapers.

One of the big shocks when you hire someone to work with you is that *they actually expect to do your work.* It was easy when you worked for a big company, but this is *your* business we're talking about now. You have to learn how to delegate, teach them what to do, and trust them to do it as well as you do. Then be prepared to redo it at 4:00 A.M., if necessary.

11. Keep your client happy, but try not to become their confidante or best friend. Don't get hooked into their personal lives beyond what you can afford. Any client (or his/her boss) can decide at any moment in time that your services are no longer necessary. You can't afford to depend on one client to the point that your business would suffer if they told you to take a hike, although this can happen more easily than you realize. Don't place a whole lot of faith in a contract; if someone wants to be rid of you, they'll find a way. Avoid giving clients expensive gifts; it can look like you charge too much money for your services. A few pounds of your famous fudge at Christmastime will mean a lot more than you think.

12. There are a bajillion federal forms you will have to

fill out for the smooth operation of your business. You'll need to file for a federal employer identification number, which will show up on every tax form you handle. There are monthly, quarterly, and annual forms to keep track of, some that make sense, others that are ridiculous.

13. I don't want to scare you or anything, but our nation's economic stability really all hangs on you, the small, decent, enterprising business owner.

Whether you have or haven't read *Be the Boss,* you really have to read *Be the Boss II.* There are all new secrets here that the first book didn't cover: stuff about electronic equipment that can shoot your business way out in front of the competition; tips on simple things you can do to help cut back on waste and save money at the same time; info on who's working at home and how you can join their ranks; how to give the best service, which will cause people to beat down your door to get you to work with them; and a whole lot more.

Now you're ready to plunge right into this second book, which is jam-packed with lots of new, exciting, and hopefully funny secrets about continuing to run your small service business in the electric, eclectic, ecologically aware, and economical 1990s. Enjoy!

Secret #147 You might want to bring along a motion sickness bag for the jerk in back of you.

Step right up folks, for the ride of your life. It's the unpredictably thrill-packed, incredible, super-duper, Great All-American Entrepreneur Rollercoaster!

But let me warn you—where it goes, *nobody knows*.

Sometime in the early 1980s, this wild thing started chugging uphill, gaining strength, numbers, and respectability as it climbed. Financial experts called it an economic expansion. The president hailed it as the age of the entrepreneur. Magazines analyzed the trend, and television sitcoms picked up the theme.

And guys named Bucky stood up near the top of the ride and raised their arms.

More new small businesses were started in the decade ending with 1990 than at any other time in U.S. history. Millions and millions of us took that leap of faith and got on for the ride. By the start of the nineties, small business represented nearly half of the Gross National Product (GNP).

Small corporations were started on a shoestring, and on $500,000 bank loans. Men, women, and teenagers of all sizes, creeds, age groups, and colors were starting their own companies. Many decided to bag the high overhead and run their businesses from home. All types of companies offering every conceivable kind of service (and some not so conceivable) fed our voracious economy the business taxes and revenues it craved.

Then the Great All-American Entrepreneur Rollercoaster

reached the crest and began to zoom downhill, along with many other businesses in the United States.

Banks went bust. Capital choked up. Small business owners defaulted on loans and debts, causing other small companies to drown. Everyone was affected by budget cutbacks, especially the contractors of services to larger companies.

And guys named Bucky puked all over the complete ride. So okay. We've had a few setbacks.

Many people learned some tough lessons from those years of unparalleled growth, and everyone who is still around has developed survival skills that would make a cockroach envious. We are keenly aware that the time when starting and running a small business might have been easy is long gone, along with the idea that it's great to drape yourself in fur while you enjoy veal piccata and put together a terrific real estate investment scheme with junk bonds.

We're leaner, meaner, and tougher to take down now. We no longer expect to have great accounts fall into our laps because of our connections, or that anyone can collect money for doing nothing (called "media commissions" back in the old days).

What we do have at our fingertips is opportunity, raw and brilliant, as did our ancestors, those brave women and men who traveled here, whether by choice or by force, and built a new world. They had the opportunity to think of new approaches to problems and of ways to offer good service and build better products for a world in need of these things.

Incredibly, the idea of giving good service has emerged from the ashes of burned out businesses to become one of the corporate world's most heralded new ideas. Even big business owners have discovered that this is a good gimmick to help attract and hold onto customers.

The riders of the Great All-American Entrepreneur Rollercoaster are alive and kicking, full of life and promise, eager to crash through the doors to what promises to be the most exciting time ever in history to start a new business, undaunted by the challenge of success or the fear of failure.

Desperate and daring, that's what we are. (Okay, more desperate than daring.)

It's not going to be easy. You want easy, go join the SEALs. You want the thrill of a lifetime, get on this track called your own business.

Whoa—what is this coming up directly ahead? OH NO—NO WAY—LOOK OUT—IT'S ANOTHER ONE! AAAAGGGGHHHHH!

Secret #148 What you need to start your own business.

For your small business, the one you've dreamed about and planned for and wanted to do most of your life, the following ingredients are essential:

1. Courage.

2. Faith in yourself.

3. Energy (either lots of the natural kind, or keep stashes of chocolate bars and pasta around).

4. Money, but certainly not a fortune. Enough to cover your expenses for six months to a year wouldn't hurt, unless you have kids, in which case you must have enough money or be able to make enough on the side to take care of them. Children and pets should never go hungry for any reason, including for your dream. You alone get to enjoy that particular pleasure.

5. A commitment to do it better, go farther, make people happier with your service or product. This reflects an intense desire burning inside you, the one that says you want to be doing this more than you ever could want to be working for someone else.

There is one more item that you may or may not need:

6. A touch of cold-bloodedness. You probably won't know whether or not you even have this in you unless it should become apparent that you could use it. Please don't get me wrong—I don't mean that you should do anything illegal or unethical. But there may

be a time when you have to make a choice, and you are going to hate your options.

Don't lose any sleep wondering how you'll know. When and if you need to use it, you'll know it.

If you use it when you don't absolutely have to, then your nose will turn green and your hair will fall out overnight.

Working in Your Home

Secret #149 Guess who's working at home.

Practically everyone you know.

Since the early 1980s, the number of people who work at home, whether running their own business or telecommuting for their employer, has gone ballistic. *The Washington Post,* (April 25, 1991) reports that according to New York City-based Link Resources Corp., a research firm, 34.8 million women and men, well over a quarter of the nation's work force of 122.7 million, are working at home. One conservative estimate from Link is that this number is projected to top 40 million before the end of this decade. Think of all those people wearing sweats or shorts instead of suits, walking from the kitchen to the den instead of power walking between the train and the office, looking out at a garden or a balcony instead of a busy, bus-clogged street. These people include full-time and part-time self-employed workers, corporate workers, freelancers, contractors, and telecommuters.

An article in *Time* (January 6, 1992) focused on the astounding number of official new businesses formed in 1991, up nearly 9% from 1980 to 1.3 million. This is how Americans respond to a recession. Nearly half of those start-ups were sole proprietorships or businesses with no more than two employees operating out of a spare room, garage, or basement, and referred to as *microbusinesses,* one of those words that you will hear or read 12 times in the next few weeks.

Sarah and Paul Edwards, who run a variety of information service enterprises from their Santa Monica, California, home, believe that many people are not finding gratification at a certain stage in life and are trying to fulfill themselves by starting a business.

"Tens of thousands of home businesses are being started by people who are simply creating a job for themselves that they cannot find or did not choose to find in a company setting," says Paul.

People have always done it, of course—craftspeople, artists, musicians, writers, the president of the United States, salespersons, and other weirdos, but due to zoning restrictions and public perception, not too many people talked about it. Now we've come out of the closet and into the mainstream.

Some of the factors that have created this phenomenal trend include:

- The computer and printer
- The fax machine
- The modem
- Federal Express, UPS, DHL, and other overnight, door-to-door, cross-continent, international (and interplanetary is the next to come, no doubt) delivery services
- Telephone equipment that makes the old black rotary dial model look like it was designed by cave dwellers
- The fact that the dog *hates* it when you leave for work
- People all across America—every shape, size, race, religion and personality—have realized, at last, that most office coffee tastes like something that came out of a sewer. This reason alone probably accounts for the mass movement toward home offices. (I'm still trying to document this through an official government agency, so don't quote me on it just yet.)

Secret #150 Psssst—it might help if you're a woman.

The average person who works at home is a woman, 39 years old, who is part of a dual-career household that earns about $42,000 a year and watches "Knots Landing."

Right now you are probably asking yourself two questions: "What has caused this tremendous increase in women home workers?" and "Is Abby Ewing ever going to return from Japan?" To answer the first question:

1. An unusually large number of women in their late 20s, 30s, and early 40s have finally acquired the job experience and self-confidence to realize that they can carve out the time necessary to care for their families, have babies, and work at a successful career by running a business out of their home.

2. It's a well-known fact that women are used to working their butts off, as we have been doing ever since someone pointed out to us that we have butts.

3. Small, successful businesses that were started in the 1980s have traditionally tapped into the pool of home-based workers to fill their employment needs while saving money on overhead and employee benefits. Their need for dependable help is greater than ever today.

The stronger sex is the fastest-growing segment of home-based workers, accounting for an astounding 70% of all home-based sole proprietorships. The Small Business Administration estimates that a woman's chance of making a new business work is about five times greater than a man's. Women, who owned about five million businesses in the United States as of 1991, are expected to own half of all small businesses in America by the end of this century, according to the SBA's Office of Advocacy.

To answer the second question, as soon as Abby decides that "Knots Landing" is the place to make her next billion dollars.

Secret #151 Hey, nobody told me about Connie's going-away luncheon at the Quality Inn.

Working from your home can lead to problems, particularly the big one of isolation, of being cut off from that fabulous office coffee and its attendant social network. Not everyone is cut out for this. Some people find that they need more supervision, more discipline.

For home workers who may run up against this, the most important steps are to admit that you're missing something, recognize what it is that you're missing, and stay involved with people and events.

Schedule frequent telephone or in-person meetings. Get dressed up and go out to meet with other people once in a while, or schedule a consultation or meeting around a business lunch or dinner. Join business groups and associations to keep informed. Take business trips with your clients, at your expense, preferably to San Francisco or Hawaii. Attend seminars, trade shows, and other fun stuff cleverly disguised as a business-related event that is also tax deductible.

Some people don't miss other workers so much as they miss knowing what is going on, and they can feel left out of it all. You may miss getting the inside information, or that esprit de corps that you were lucky enough to have at your former office. Keep in close contact with the office gossip, the one who knows about the birthdays and going-away parties and baby showers. You may need help or support when you're dealing with a rough job or assignment. You may need to bounce ideas off of colleagues. Invite people over to your office to consult, or just kick thoughts around. Serve donuts and coffee, or club soda and cheeses.

Working at home should not mean you are in prison for the rest of your life. Do whatever you have to do to keep yourself included in the parts you miss.

Secret #152 Okay, who took the last fudge-covered Oreo?

There can be other small problems when you work out of your home.

For one thing, you could quickly balloon up to 500 pounds, if you're not careful, and get asked to be the main attraction in your town's next float parade.

You're just going along, working on billings or doing some project, and suddenly the letter "G" leaps at your face, reminding you of Girl Scout Cookies, of which you have four boxes stashed away on the top shelf above the stove in the kitchen.

The kitchen with its full fridge and stocked cabinets. Milky Way mecca. Nacho nirvana. Sandwich shangri-la.

Some people avoid going into the kitchen area all day by installing coffeemakers and little fridges in their office area, and others discipline themselves by chaining a limb to the desk. I won't insult your intelligence by telling you to just keep busy. Everyone knows that the busier you are, the more food you need to keep up that energy level.

If you're the type of person who thinks about food only between meals, you could try to make it very hard to get into the kitchen by installing a lock on the door to the den of temptation and tossing the key up onto a bookcase shelf, or you could put up a poster of the thin, ravishingly gorgeous person whom you would like to resemble.

If these things don't work, buy bigger clothes.

All this talk about food has made me hungry, so excuse me while I go have a snack.

Secret #153 "Hold on a sec, I dropped my Hermes scarf."

Some people who feel funny about working out of their homes use clothing tricks to help convince themselves that they're working in a real office in order to keep up that image of the professional.

They get dressed in a business outfit every morning, drive around the block, park, get out, come in the side entrance, and open up the office. Great. Whatever gets you going. However, if I had to do all that, I'd at least keep a pair of jeans and a big old sweatshirt in the office and change the instant I got there.

Even though most people would like to wear jeans or sweats to work, there are some who don't feel professional in these casual things, which is the wonderful thing about working at home. You can wear a $1,500 suit every day. Or you can wear a diamond tiara and your kid's Halloween Darth Vader outfit, as long as you don't mind the looks you get from the water-meter reader and the exterminator and the couriers and your accountant, who just happened to drop by with your year-end statement.

The important thing is to sound as though you are dressed well. And don't ever buy a video telephone.

Secret #154 (Now where was I?)

Another problem is that of concentration, if you're prone to be distracted (did I lock that window?) by thoughts of outside things (did I feed the dog?) now and then.

What you have to learn (where's that siren noise coming from?) to do is to apply all your self-discipline (it's down at the corner! gotta go look) to learn how to stay at your desk, filter out noises (I can't believe that witch across the street is riding her stationary bike in the window like that in that teeny tiny eeny weeny little body suit, plus she's so skinny, like she *needs* to exercise, yeah, right) and other distractions, and keep working until the job (she's 40 if she's a day, and that boyfriend of hers can't be a minute over 25) is done.

Force yourself to focus on your work. Look around your office. It's really a mess, isn't it? Which leads us to another problem of working out of your home.

Secret #155 Oh, *gross*—what is this in the corner?

If your office is a total wreck, you'll probably pick up your spirits and feel more in control if you take the time to clean it. Some people thrive on sloppy work areas, but if you are the type who likes to feel organized, it's important to clean up the joint now and then.

Put old files away, remove bodies of small rodents, break down jobs and store the papers out of sight, keep your desk in somewhat manageable shape, replace light bulbs that have burned out, and while you're at it, dust and sweep back here once in a blue moon, just as the night crew did at your old office.

(Did you know that a blue moon isn't really blue? I think it's when there are two full moons within one calendar month. Somebody let me know if this is wrong so I won't go the rest of my life thinking this is what it is.)

Cleaning up will do wonders for your peace of mind and sense of order, plus now that the dustballs are gone, you have room for another filing cabinet over in that corner, in which you can have a secret cache of peanut butter crackers and Fifth Avenue candy bars.

Secret #156 To bark or not to bark.

And then there are children and pets. These smaller-than-normal creatures can make life in the home office hectic, if not downright horrible. Kids you can bribe with cash and credit cards, but pets are something else.

Barking dogs are great for getting rid of potential burglars and those equally pesky salespeople who drop by with samples. But not everyone finds it as adorable as you do, so you should remove all barky dogs from your work area if you deal with clients over the phone. Quiet dogs are okay, but the instant there's a cat on the windowsill outside, your placid dog may turn your office into bark city.

Speaking of cats, we had one visiting once when we happened to be trying to land a small part of the Xerox Corp. account. Cats are sweet little things; they don't do a whole lot except sleep and eat and go exploring in the backyard, right?

They also decide to leap onto your lap when you're talking on the phone to this guy who's head of marketing, and you are so startled that you drop the phone, not just on the desk, but all the way onto the floor where it clatters against the side of the desk, which makes you laugh hysterically at everything.

The guy had three cats of his own, and he seemed to understand and even laughed at the whole terrible episode with me.

We did not get the account.

I ate moon pies and Fritos for days.

Secret #157 It was a dark and stormy night.

If you decide to invest in a computer for your home office (see the next chapter, "Ready or Not, Welcome to the Electronic Age"), you'll want to protect it as much as you can. Buy a surge protector for those rooms where you have your heavy equipment. It's about as big as a box of spaghetti, with several outlets along one side, and it protects your equipment from most temper tantrums that the power supply can throw.

Don't let anybody sell you on the notion that these surge protectors can guard your equipment from lightning. Nothing, and I mean *nothing* except your wits, can protect your equipment if your home or a transformer or the telephone pole connected to your home is struck by lightning.

If you live in an area where spring and summer electrical storms are about as commonplace as kids with popsicles, as we do, then clean out your ears and listen for the distant sound of thunder. If you hear it, save your work, shut down immediately, and *pull the plug from the outlet*. Lightning can zap through phone lines just as easily as electrical wires, so if you have a modem, make sure you disconnect its incoming telephone line or disconnect the cable. Try to get in the habit of doing this at night after you finish working, too, during storm season.

Then go have your margarita by the hurricane lamp.

Secret #158 Are you legal?

If you're running a business from your home, apartment, or condo, and you don't know where you should call to find out whether or not you're allowed to be running this business, you're probably not legal. But don't lose any sleep. Hardly anyone working at home is legal.

Zoning commissions are set up in many cities, counties, and municipalities. But some places, Houston, for example, don't have zoning laws. Zoning laws serve perfectly good purposes in that they try to keep a lid on undesirable, noisy businesses and uncontrolled growth, as well as protect the privacy of everyone (so you won't ever have to look out your front window one morning and wonder why Earl poured all that concrete over his grass, and why he put up that sign that reads "Learn to Power Jackhammer in 20 Easy Lessons").

If you want to be a really good citizen, call the zoning administration in your area and ask what the restrictions are, if any, on running a small business out of one room of a home, or get a copy of the ordinances and read them, or ask a lawyer.

If, however, you are like most business owners in that you don't want any more hassles than you already have, the buzzword here is low, as in profile. Don't give your neighbors any reason to complain about you. Don't put up a huge neon sign with arrows pointing to your side entrance. Don't operate any heavy machinery or have a lot of odors or sounds coming from your business. Don't have a constant stream of couriers and visitors. Don't dump gravel in the street or alley. And above all, make sure no one sees you reading this page. You wouldn't believe what I went through to make sure no one saw me writing it.

Actually, I just remembered that I didn't write it. This

part was written by a mystery guest author whose name I cannot divulge, but who is at this moment sneaking around Earl's house winding toilet paper all over that new sign of his.

Secret #159 Cease and desist, or you might lose ShowMaxBO.

If someone complains about your business to the zoning commission, you are going to have a problem. They have the power to make you stop faster than you would if you were driving along and saw someone gorgeous and naked walking on the sidewalk. (Oh, like you wouldn't stop. You lie.)

Here's what can happen to you if someone reports you.

1. You could receive a notice that orders you to stop operating your business, now. They don't mean next month or next week—they mean now.

2. If you don't stop, they could get a court order to make you stop.

3. If you don't obey the court order, you're in contempt of court, and you can be fined or thrown into the slammer.

4. If you still don't stop, you could have something really horrible happen to you, like they could scramble your premium cable channels and *not tell you*.

Before it gets this far, do something positive. Take some action. It's the American way.

You do have a few options in addition to keeping the low profile. For one thing, you could change your business so that you comply with any zoning restrictions in your area. If you're violating the number of pickups and drop-offs allowed, you could have a drop-off place at a nearby Mail Boxes or business office for your couriers and mail.

Second, you could apply for a use permit, which means

that official people would come and investigate your home and decide whether or not this setup is okay. At least you can avoid being dragged out in front of a town council or some such thing.

If you like the idea of being dragged out in front of a town council, you could apply for a variance, or exception to the rule, our third suggestion. You'd have to be the star at a public hearing and explain why you deserve to be singled out, why your business is different from everyone else's.

One other option is to get involved in your local political scene and try to get the laws changed. When Washington, D.C.'s city council was leaning toward imposing heavy restrictions on small businesses run from private homes, a town meeting was held. All the members of the small business community were invited to attend and express their views.

There were so many people at the first meeting, there weren't enough chairs. More meetings were scheduled, and even more people showed up. After several professional people testified and many more requested to testify, council members realized they had a big mess on their hands. Seemed as though there were more people in D.C. working out of their homes than there were government employees.

The original complaint had involved bed-and-breakfast inns tucked into the tiny, picturesque streets of the nation's capital. Actually, the complaints were from neighbors of the B&Bs about the many cars with out-of-state plates trying to find parking spaces on those same tiny, picturesque streets, and the residents had no place to tuck their cars when they came home from work at night.

To everyone's relief, a compromise was reached about the number of visitor cars allowed to park on the street, and all the dentists and doctors and consultants and lawyers drove back to their home offices, where there were no parking spaces available.

And we all lived happily ever after.

Secret #160 Get it in writing.

Okay, so you're zoned and licensed for business. What else do you need? Sit down.

If you're going to have anything to do with food, from selling grilled hot dogs on the street corner to catering magnificent meals for dinner parties, you are going to become best pals with the Food and Drug Administration and your local health department. The preparation and selling of food is one of the most closely regulated businesses in the complete universe, which is wonderful or horrible, depending on whether you are consuming or preparing. You can pretty much count on seeing the health inspectors more than you might want to, as well as members of your local fire department who may want to inspect your home, and even people from special occupancy agencies who might want to take a tour.

Are you sure you want to get into the food business? Alright. First thing you need to do is write to this place:

> The Food and Drug Administration
> Division of Regulatory Guidance (HFF-314)
> 200 C Street, S.W.
> Washington, D.C. 20204

Or call the helpful people at FDA's Center for Food Safety and Applied Nutrition at 202/485-0187 (in Washington, D.C.). Explain what type of food business you want to operate, and ask for any information they can send you. Another place you should contact is your local city or county Board of Health.

If your food business has anything to do with desserts in general, or chocolate in particular, you could send me a sample of everything you'd like to have professionally evaluated.

State governments feel left out if you don't tell them what you're doing. Before you can legally earn a living in many kinds of occupations or perform any type of service on the human or animal body, most states require you to pass an exam and obtain a license.

If you want to broadcast a radio or television program from your living room, or give advice on investments, or do any meat processing (three professions that obviously are linked closely), you will probably need a federal license. Call the Federal Trade Commission to find out their requirements.

Other types of permits that you may need to apply for in this environmentally aware age we live in include air- and water-pollution control permits, especially if you're going to be burning any material, or using gas-producing stuff like paint sprayers, or storing caustic or toxic chemicals of any type (the fire department likes to know about this), or if you're discharging anything into your sewers other than normal human waste.

Secret #161 Where in the world will you go today?

While sipping your first cup of coffee, you browsed through the morning newspaper, placed a book order, selected wine to be delivered for your dinner party, bought clothes, checked your mail, wrote letters and posted them to your friends, looked up a type of medication and its side effects, discovered which sonnet had that quote you heard last night, found out the population and average annual rainfall of Mauritius, checked the singles classified ads to see how many people are wanting to meet left-handed transvestites who were formerly dancing dwarf nuns, and you attended a conference.

You stood up, stretched, then checked to see if Count Chockula in Atlanta had responded to your cryptic message, booked your pretend itinerary to Europe and Japan, read the State Department's briefing about which countries to avoid travel-wise speaking, looked to see if the price for your dream car was under $50,000, ordered designer chocolates sent to your Valentine (it's August), and sold some stock.

Before lunch, you scoped out the new rarest disease in the world, read about some of the problems and pleasures experienced by people who work out of their homes, made your move in SNIPER!, got caught up on the soaps in Tinseltown, which reminded you to order a gift basket of soaps to be sent to your aunt for her birthday, downloaded a photo of a naked man (which your aunt would probably rather have), ran a credit check on yourself, peeked at the latest list of U.S. government publications, and absorbed news from the scuba world.

And you never left your house.

With a computer, telephone, and modem (see the next chapter if you don't know what a modem is), you can do anything. Through the awesome (I'm allowed to use that word three times in this book) capabilities of online services such as CompuServe, America Online, and Prodigy, we have indeed become a global village, just as Alvin Toffler predicted in *The Third Wave*. The scope and depth of possibilities available to each of us from our home is far greater than most of us ever envisioned, except for that nerdy kid named Crandall with whom we all went to school and who built his own computer and designed a program that enabled him to travel to the future while the rest of us were stuck in tenth grade.

Electronic information services have changed the way we live and work, saving us a fortune in parking and traveling costs along the way. Remember back in the seventies when we were all petrified of using an automatic teller machine? Now we're so used to zipping up to our cutely named money machine and getting cash quickly that we can't stand to go inside a bank for any reason.

Network communication systems are in the process of changing the way we do just about everything else. So far, over half a million of us have gotten hooked by these electronic centers of information, but you can bet they won't stop until there are as many subscribers as there are personal computers.

The dastardly way they go about this is by offering competitive prices and free sign-ups, giving you more choices, adding on more things for you to do and enjoy and explore. There are over 7,000 of these databases just a phone call away from you. For a nominal startup fee, you get a kit that describes how to sign up and tells you which options are available (some have executive plans, along with your plans ordinaire), a monthly magazine for members, and possibly a credit toward usage time. Then once you start using the service, you are billed for the minutes that you are connected by modem, plus they'll probably stick on a small monthly fee.

One invaluable feature is the electronic reference libraries. You can quickly look up stuff in the encyclopedia, find facts from scientific, legal, literary, medicinal, and other reference sources, or search for articles from a number of publications.

Here are some phone numbers of a few of the larger information vendors:

CompuServe, 513/223-6876
Dialog Information Services, Inc., 415/858-2700
Dow Jones News/Retrieval, 609/520-4000
Mead Data Central, 513/864-7200
NewsNet, Inc., 800/334-0329

And then there are BBSs (bulletin board systems). Like the big commercial ones, a BBS will provide you with plenty of information and people who can answer your questions, as well as offer the most up-to-the-minute versions of neat stuff you can download, or pull into your computer, such as public domain (you can use it without having to pay), and shareware software (which is a program you can try, then pay for, if you decide you like it enough to keep it).

There are all types of BBSs, and most of them are free! You have to pay for any long distance calls, but not the time on the BBS. In the Washington, D.C. area, small business owners can get advice, find reference materials, and make contacts through Ed-Link, a local BBS provided as a service by the joint efforts of Montgomery County High Technology Council and Montgomery College Small Business Development Center. This BBS is set up so that you can join on-going discussions in at least a dozen categories of interest, as well as find out about courses at colleges and small business development centers in the D.C. area.

You can find out about BBSs in or near your area by calling your local office of the Small Business Administration, or through your computer store or dealer, schools and universities, or just by asking around, especially people who have a system like yours.

P.S. Although it's not possible to list all the BBSs in this country because there are so many, you could find several of them in *The Macintosh Bible*. It's an indispensable, well-written, beautifully organized, entertaining, and perfectly marvelous tool if you have a Macintosh computer.

Secret #162   Everybody needs to belong to something.

There are associations for people who run a business from home, as well as several for small business owners in general. These groups distribute information to their members from experts on such topics as taxes and legal advice, and most of them offer benefits including insurance and travel discounts, assuming that you not only have time to join, but to actually take a trip somewhere.

> American Federation of Small Business
> 407 S. Dearborn Street
> Chicago, IL 60605-1115
> Phone: 312/427-0206

These guys are big—there are 25,000 members; they promote free enterprise and oppose big government and labor monopoly, and they had their annual meeting in Hawaii in 1990, which makes me want to join.

> National Association for the Cottage Industry
> P.O. Box 14460
> Chicago, IL 60614
> Phone: 312/472-8116

Owners of home-based businesses or individuals who work at flexible or remote work sites comprise this membership. NACI publishes "Mind Your Own Business at Home" bi-monthly and a quarterly, "The Cottage Connection."

National Association for the Self-Employed
P.O. Box 612067
Dallas, TX 75261
Phone: 800/232-6273
Fax: 817/595-5456

Friendly in the way that Texans are. Costs $48 to join. You can call someone named the Shop Talking Gentleman from 8 A.M. to 12 noon (CST) Monday through Friday and ask any questions about running your own small business.

Small Business Council of America
4800 Hampden Lane, 7th Floor
Bethesda, MD 20814
Phone: 301/656-7603

These people are primarily into representing the federal tax and employee benefit interests of their members to prevent federal tax laws from swallowing them up. Sounds good to me.

See the sixth chapter, "How to Find Work, Where to Get Help," for information on Small Business Development Centers (SBDCs) located at or near most state universities and colleges everywhere, brought to you courtesy of those most excellent people at the Small Business Administration.

Ready or Not, Welcome to the Electronic Age

Secret #163 It's a wizzywig world.

Okay. You've given this a lot of thought. You want to run a successful, competitive service business, make a little bit of money, and enjoy some free time, and you realize that a computer might help you achieve these goals.

Just as that first journey you ever made in your life, the trip from the womb to the outside world, was such a complete and total shock, so this one is going to be.

Everything is different today from how it used to be back in the pre-all-electronic age: the way to keep records, the way to keep clients, the way to keep costs down. The way to keep some kind of grip on your sanity.

With the possible exception of most agencies of the federal government, a few publishing companies in New York City, and my dermatologist, nobody relies on filing cabinets with manila folders stuffed with carbon copies of typed letters anymore. This type of office went out with the old "Ann Sothern" show, which was out before Elvis was originally seen alive in the mid-fifties when he actually was alive.

Now if you're a complete genius, or a ten-year-old kid who has played Tetris nonstop since you were in diapers, this is going to be a snap.

For most of the rest of us, it's not simple or easy. Learning these new ropes takes a lot of time and effort, and it really helps to have an on-site expert with you at all times, such as the 10-year-old Tetris player.

But if you put your mind to it, you can do it.

You'll learn new terms like pixel, dpi, and wysiwyg (sounds like wizzywig), explore incredible ways of doing things faster than you ever imagined, find yourself working late at something you sort of enjoy, and you just might get good enough at video games to beat your bratty little nephew next Thanksgiving.

So grab a 10-pound bag of Oreos or Doritos or whatever, curl up, and read on. This is the easy part.

Secret #164 Anyone can learn how to use a computer.

Whether you're old, young, smart, stupid, fast, slow, weird, witty, busy, boring, rich, poor, tall, thin, ugly, or uncommonly beautiful, these things have nothing to do with it.

What has *everything* to do with it is your attitude.

Your ability to learn is only limited by the size of the blinders you put on yourself. You don't have to be mechanically inclined, or be able to leap tall buildings in a single bound, or be so obviously brilliant that people whisper as you pass. (People whisper as I pass, but it's usually because of the big run in my pantyhose or the toilet paper stuck to my shoe.)

You work with computers every day. The average American home has 11 computers in it. Every time you make popcorn in your microwave, use a calculator to add up all that interest you earned on your certificates of deposit, set up your answering machine to tape phone calls, reset your security system, or program your VCR to tape "America's Most Rich and Famous Full House of the Dark Shadows in 48 Hours," you are using a computer. You don't have to understand how these things work—you only need to know how to use them.

Using a computer for business is exactly the same thing.

Preschoolers in Georgetown, Kentucky, are learning colors, numbers, and the alphabet on the computers in their community daycare center before they have a nap.

A popular program sponsored by many grocery stores around the country enables schools to get free computers by collecting enough receipt slips, and millions of children and teens are eagerly learning how to use these computers while parents are standing outside grocery stores, begging people for their receipts.

One of my best friends in the world, let's call him Rick, came across an offer at his bank a few years ago—a free Mac Plus if he rolled over a savings certificate. He didn't type or draw, and he wasn't sure if he had any use for a computer, but he decided to take advantage of it anyway.

Rick set up a system that keeps track of all his checking and savings account information, pays his bills, and balances his statements; he organized all of the personal and household information, learned a word-processing program so he could write letters to friends and family, helped his wife Aida (another of my best friends in the world) set up a file for her vast recipe collection, as well as learn the word-processing program so she could write anything from a letter to a book; he learned Hypercard, which is a masterful filing program; he got a modem, which enabled him to hook up with a computer service that offers all sorts of information and programs; and his idea of a fun thing to do is to spend a rainy afternoon reading *The Macintosh Bible*.

Rick has a birth certificate that turned 79 years old in 1993.

Secret #165   This must be the "ON" switch.

If you already know how computers can help your business, congratulations—you're a winner.

If you're not sure or really don't have a clue about how a computer can help you run your business, you are about to be incredibly, wonderfully surprised, as well as become a winner.

Computers have truly revolutionized how we write, design, plot, plan, predict, simulate, keep records of expenses, compile data for billings, sort through mountains of facts and details, work out charts and graphs, make sense of all the information that is at our fingertips, and have some fun.

With a computer, a telephone, and a modem (See Secret #173 to find out all about modems, but don't bother because you'll be there in a few minutes anyway), you have the capability of offering a whole new world of services to your clients so inexpensively that they won't believe their luck. And neither will you.

Practically every small business can benefit from a computer. Having one usually can mean the difference between being frantic because you haven't gotten the billings or the proposal or the figures done, and being able to enjoy a few free hours each week doing those extra, small things you enjoy—such as eating and sleeping.

If you can afford it, buy one.

If you can't afford it, buy one anyway.

Get the best computer you can for your type of business. This will take a bit of research on your part, but once you get into it, it can be kind of fun. (Okay, so I lead a dull life.) If possible, find someone else in your business and ask what type of equipment they have (nobody says "hardware'' anymore, except as in ''I'm going to the hardware store to buy a rake''). At a computer store or library, you can find literally tons of magazines and books that have current information about which computer is best for your small business.

Or I can simplify your search somewhat: get a Macintosh if you're an artist or do desktop publishing. Buy an IBM if you write or do spreadsheets or charts.

That's pretty much the heart of it.

Secret #166   Remember who signs the checks.

It does not necessarily follow that the more complex your business needs are, the more money you'll need to fork over for a computer. There are some wonderful computers in lower price ranges that do a lot of neat stuff, and if you're ferret-like about it, you can find them.

The goal of the computer salesperson, however, is to upsell* you when you walk in the door. After all, computer companies have spent enough money to buy the entire universe and property in Japan in order just to advertise the fact that they have developed the technology capable of covering every business need, whether it's two letters a year or 800 billion skillion jillion manuscripts. They've got to try and make it back somehow.

So you might notice a bit of overkill when you walk into your friendly neighborhood computer store, where you will describe to whichever salesperson, who manages to kill everyone else first in order to get to you, exactly what you think you need with a computer.

Appearing to listen politely, he or she will then show you the newest, most awesome, most completely all-encompassing computer ever made and try to convince you that you must have this top-of-the-line model because of the phenomenal way your company is going to grow, and they'll have to run in the back and check on this, but they think that yes—it just happens to be the last three minutes that this particular model is on sale at this incredibly low

*Please don't tell anyone I used the nonword "upsell," which is the computer term for when someone tries to sell you something costing more than what you intended to pay.

price, and they'll also throw in free software that allows you to go to Saturn.

Pry yourself away and look around. Find a model that's not a souped-up turbo, preferably one that costs less than your house or condo. This shouldn't be too hard. Ask for a demonstration of one that you like, even though the salesperson wants you to buy the awesome model so he or she can retire to St. Croix. Take your time. Walk out of the store. Think about it.

You might even find, when you come back the next day or so, that the salesperson has asked the manager if it's okay to throw in something free or at cost, just because you're such a nice person.

Secret #167 Pack your pixels.

It's practically impossible to commit to buying a computer because of one simple fact: *they're always coming out with a newer version in about two minutes.*

And this newer one will do everything that the older ones will do in one-third of the time, take up only half the space, comes with a larger screen, more colors, more pixels (which means dots) per square inch to give you better resolution, plus it walks your dog. But keep this in mind as you're hearing about the newer one—something usually happens, as in big problem, to block its appearance on the market for a while. Even if it's there in front of you, winking and blinking each one of its gorgeous pixels at you, you can count on the newer version of anything to probably have bugs or kinks in it for a while—bugs or kinks that might make your system come crashing down around you one day.

Several designers we know had each installed an upgraded design program at about the same time, used it for a few weeks, then on the same afternoon experienced that peculiar form of terror that people who depend on computers know is always possible; their computers went haywire and they had to shut down.

Another time, a colleague of ours was having terrific headaches which began on the same day that she started using her new, super-expensive, tiltable, swiveling, 19-inch color monitor. She had her eyeglass prescription checked and her lenses adjusted, and she saw a doctor about treatment for migraines. Then one day, she realized that the top part of her new monitor was fuzzy. When she tried to adjust it, another part went skewy.

A technician at the store where she had bought it told her that this type of monitor can be out of focus by 2 to

5%, and if this was causing her headaches, that the only way to avoid them was to not look at that part of the monitor that was fuzzy.

We try not to be in a huge hurry to move up to a new program or be the first kid on the block to buy an untested model, just as when a restaurant opens, you want to wait a few weeks or months until the staff and kitchen have worked out the hair-in-the-soup problems.

Secret #168   Come on in, the water's freezing.

Some of us have the luxury of going to a computer learning school, or of being taught a computer program on the job by someone who knows it and is a good teacher.

And some of us get tossed in the icy cold waters to flounder around for ourselves.

The second way, under a deadline crunch to get a manuscript to my editor, is how I learned WordPerfect, a word-processing program for the IBM-PC. I've done more fun things in my life.

No one has ever accused me of being a technical genius, not by any stretch. The way I program the VCR to tape a show that comes on an hour from now is I go to the microwave, set the timer for 55 minutes, and then when it beeps, this reminds me that I have five minutes to find the channel on the television, put a tape in the VCR, and press "Record."

So to sit in front of a computer, only sure of where the "On/Off" switch was located, and learn WordPerfect so that I could finish the manuscript on time was, for me, a challenge. Especially considering the way the manuals were written back then in the early eighties.

Many of the guidebooks that help you learn the programs today are much better written and illustrate everything clearly. They make those manuals of the late seventies and early eighties look like they were written in some Nancy Drew or Hardy Boys secret code. Plus, once you successfully turn on and get into any of the Mac computers, you can take these nifty guided tours through the basic commands and begin to grasp what you are going to be able to do.

We bought a program called Quicken for paying bills and keeping checkbook records. This is the most marvelous program, and I'm sure there are many others just as marvelous out there. With Quicken, I record all of our transactions, write checks, maintain a check/deposit ledger, code each type of transaction for our accountant so he can do our books more efficiently, print out complete records, and I can even balance the checkbook statement each month. But setting it all up didn't just happen overnight.

First, every vendor, supplier, and other business to which we send checks had to be entered into the master list; I entered the name, address, monthly amount (if it was constant), and code for this type of expenditure.

Okay, no problem, I thought, gathering my bills so I could start.

Several hours later, with all the interruptions of a busy office, I'd only done a dozen or so checks because I was logging in all the information about each company as I went. Plus there was a lot about Quicken that I was looking up along the way. The next time I did checks, more new places were added to the master list, but it was easier. And after that, it got even faster.

Now it takes me only a few minutes to write, record and print out checks.

Try and set aside a couple of weeks or a month to learn any new program, and set it up before you rely on using it in your business. You'll learn a few shortcuts and devise some others on your own. You'll call the store where you bought the program, plus some 800 toll-free numbers now and then to ask questions. Be prepared to screw up or even lose some work because of a mistake. You'll hate everything about computers, and you'll hate me for writing that you could do it.

But there will also be that time when you sit back and congratulate yourself for figuring it out, you genius.

Secret #169   What the Zapf Dingbat* is electronic publishing?

Electronic publishing, or desktop publishing, or computer publishing, is one of the most revolutionary things to happen to the business world since type balls.

If your business has anything to do with the handling of information for your clients, you really have to offer this service or you might as well hang it up and move into your brother's basement. If you still use words like "mimeograph" or think that putting a report or newsletter together is a big deal, boy are you ever in the wrong century.

Electronic publishing means you can produce anything from a 40-page staff report to the boss's daughter's wedding invitation to a book-length manuscript on the screen in front of you, drop in design elements or illustrations, make changes as you go, and print out laser copies that look professional and beautiful and that are also camera-ready for a printer.

Advertising agencies, public relations firms, design studios, and other communications companies have found that electronic publishing cuts into their billings and profits, big

* Zapf Dingbat, by the way, is a typeface, or font. It has lots of neat little characters and shapes such as card suits, arrows, asterisks, brackets, boxes, geometric shapes, scissors, stars, pencils, snowflakes, and more. Another really cool one is Cairo, with its exotic, modern-day hieroglyphic symbols. The primary purpose of these fonts is that you and your friends can assign letters to each symbol and write secret letters to each other.

time. But clients don't want to pay enormous sums of money to have creative people come up with layouts on black velvet board, nor do they want to pay for the old-fashioned, expensive typesetting procedures.

It's kind of like driving from Idaho to Montana by way of Florida.

And in spite of the fact that there's always a resident writer or designer in every company, many businesses still need the assistance of a genuinely creative person, one who can see there's a great headline lurking out there beyond the first thought that pops out of the vice-president's mouth, or a terrific angle to be marketed.

Your small, information-oriented company with its low overhead that has the right kind of equipment and offers good service at low rates is perfectly positioned to make out, just like the Beagle Boys when Uncle Scrooge left the door to his vault open.

Secret #170 Pardon the expression, but are you saved?

The most important thing you must do on a computer is to
save as you go
save as you go
save as you go
because anything can happen while you're working. We've all lost important, sometimes irreplaceable
save as you go
save as you go
save as you go
files due to an error in the system, which causes a bomb, or because of a power failure in the neighborhood, or maybe
save as you go
save as you go
save as you go
the dog chews through the cord and gets a free neutering job, so
save as you go
save as you go
save as you go
(you should repeat this until ad ralpheum sets in).

Secret #171 The indispensable *fax* machine.

In case you haven't read a paper or picked up a magazine since the dinosaurs died, a fax machine is a combination telephone-copier that sends words, photos, or anything that can be copied to any other fax machine through the telephone lines.

The word *fax* is derived from the term "facsimile," which was popular during the ancient Pre-PC Office Language era, which was also noted for the Thermofax, or Qwip, machine (of which there were other similar prehistoric models). An even earlier Pre-PC device that predated "facsimile" was the "carbon copy," or the more casual "carbon." Before that, there were monks with callouses and eyestrain.

Along with the computer, the fax is the best investment our business has ever made. Practically overnight, our courier bill was cut in half, which didn't please our couriers a whole lot, but our clients loved seeing proofs in one minute instead of two to four hours later.

Not that fax copies are perfect. Hardly. On the receiving end you have to put up with lines that are sometimes squiggly, margins that are sometimes jiggly, and sudden little quirks possibly created by a telephone repair guy in Horsehide, Tennessee, who just got a free permanent wave in every hair on his body. And when the fax is moody, it can do things like get stuck on a word or phrase, dragging it all the way down the page like the longest, skinniest, most unreadable bar code in the world.

But once you've used your fax for a week, you won't be able to imagine how you got along without it. Pages of copy can be sent for you to work with. Photos that you need to see copies of, or notes that were taken, copies of receipts, reports, forms to fill out—if it can be copied, it can be sent by fax. Any business can benefit from the speed and efficiency of this little miracle of telephone technology.

And when the client says isn't that weird, but the *second* bill you mailed never arrived either, you can just fax a copy to them.

But as with everything, there can be problems.

Secret #172 Faux fax and things that go ring in the night.

Once your clients think they know that you know how they think (quick, somebody see if that's a palindrome!), you'll receive lots of little goodies by fax. Messages from a client can save plenty of time and prevent the hideous syndrome of meetingitis. Kathy has some illustration accounts for which she has never met an actual person, because layouts and approvals are transmitted by fax machine.

There are some things for which you still need original paperwork, however, like estimates, applications, authorizations, money transfers, and other legal documents that need to be signed. Practically everyone sends out and returns these forms by fax. Legally, this isn't worth the fax paper it's on (which is a solid waste problem; for helpful suggestions, see chapter eight—Environmental and recycling information).

According to the *Commercial Lending Newsletter* (August 1990), a desktop-published communique for the banking industry, even bankers have accepted fax papers as the real thing only to have been duped. Apparently, someone had a fraudulent order to transfer a huge amount of money abroad (gee, let me guess, to Switzerland?), which was "verified" by a real-looking letterhead, which had been sent by fax. Some dastardly dastard cut out the letterhead and signature from the real thing, doing a paste-and-glue job on the verification letter.

This is one way that fax fraud can be perpetrated, and if anybody reading this tries it, I'm going to personally cover you in moose dung and put you in a fly's version of Grand

Central, you got that? This book is not designed to give you ideas like that. Besides, I tried it and the glued part ripped off going through the fax machine, which cost $2,000 to fix.

The other thing you have to watch for is transmitting confidential information to someone, such as copies of contracts you want only your attorney to see, or today's "The Far Side" to your niece who works at the newspaper. Just make sure the person to whom you are sending the message knows about it and is standing there, ready to yank it out.

Once your fax number gets into circulation, however, you're headed for big trouble, as in junk fax. Junk fax is utterly worthless trash that originates from an office on something like Sunset Boulevard where no real person actually works. It's just a bunch of slave fax machines programmed to dial every fax everywhere and offer free Coffee Man.

It should be a law that if anybody sends junk fax, they have to sit in a prison cell with an incoming fax machine and receive junk fax for the complete rest of their lives, or until they snap and actually order a Coffee Man.

It's bad enough to tie up the fax line and use up your paper during the middle of the business day, but if you run your business out of your home and the fax machine uses the phone in the bedroom (kinky, but there are about 16 people who do this), you will also be aware of the messages that arrive at 2:12 A.M. Or 5:36 A.M. By the time you get the 20th piece of paper that says you can have a free vacation to the Bahamas or a free roll of fax paper for just signing away your complete business and personal life, you'll realize that you can either:

1. Call long distance, at your expense, and try to get the obnoxious person originating these messages to cease and desist;

2. Somehow get the obnoxious person's PIN code and program their fax to call Tokyo Time for a solid week; or

3. Put the fax in a place where you can't hear it at night. None of your clients would be so vulgar as to send you something by fax at night anyway.

P.S. If you unhook the fax line at night, the slave fax machines will still dial your fax number and let it ring and ring and ring until you stagger to the phone to answer, and when you do, you'll get this tone in your ear that will prevent you from hearing dog whistles and whistling dogs and in fact everything for the rest of your dog days.

P.P.S. I guess you could turn off the ringer, but what a major inconvenience to have to remember to turn it back on the next morning.

Secret #173 If your dictionary dates back to the Carter administration, it probably does not have this word in it.

Modem. Short for modulator/demodulator, which nobody in the computer world has time to say.

A modem can be an internal piece of equipment, tucked inside your hard drive, or a small box outside, connected by a cable to one of those ports in the back of your hard drive. It serves as your computer's telephone.

It was probably created by a bunch of high school kids sitting around in one of their basements, completely zonked on their parents' Aerosmith tape and Twinkies, who decided that it was a shame that computers didn't have arms and hands with which to answer a ringing phone, which was one of their neighbors calling to tell them to turn down that stupid music.

In order for your computer to be able to communicate with other computers, they each have to have a modem, too. (It is not yet known whether or not some teenage computers have pink princess modems with private numbers in their rooms.)

Every modem has to have access to a telephone line. Some places, such as the Pentagon and IBM, can afford to buy a private line just for their computer's modem. Most of us hitchhike onto a second line in our home or office, usually the same one we use for our fax machine to communicate with other fax machines. Any other computer's modem, fax, or actual person calling this line during the time that your computer spends talking with other computers will get a busy signal. And if your computer makes a long distance call, you're going to pay, Ray.

Okay. So big deal, you're thinking. My computer can call up another computer. And do what, get a stock price? Maybe the weather in Hong Kong? Like wow.

(For those of you who don't know yet, *this is so exciting!* Because you're about to get your socks blown off.)

Secret #174   How long has it been since you washed your socks?

A modem is your ticket to the world of information.

Say one of your clients works on the computer, whether at home, on the commuter bus, at the office, or sitting in the park, and he or she does a six-page report and wants you to turn it into a small brochure. There is a disk with all this copy on it, already typed by the client, who of course has a different type of computer than you have.

Traditionally, which is without a modem, you have to find a service bureau that can convert your client's disk to one that you can use in your computer, get the disk to the service bureau, wait for the technician to transfer it to your computer's format, get it delivered from the service bureau, and insert it into your computer, hoping that there won't be a virus on the disk, or a million characters that you can't make any sense out of, or an encoding procedure that has put every letter on its own line, or some other surprise.

Service bureaus charge varying fees for disk transfers, depending on whether the technician has to go into the disk and do anything to it to help make it readable, plus deliveries. (If you're asking yourself, What the heck is a service bureau? see the next secret. These places do a whole lot more than disk transfers; they are the newest, hottest shops for anyone who is into electronic publishing.)

Here's the scenario with modems: your client calls your computer, and with a few keystrokes the copy that was typed at home/bus/office/park is delivered by telephone line, directly into your computer. Six typed pages would probably take about 47 seconds, tops. No kidding. And *it's already typed.*

There are translator programs that can convert copy from one type of a computer to another type, such as IBM to Mac.

Imagine what this could mean in terms of time and money saved if your client wants you to handle a newsletter, an annual report, tons of charts and figures, a magazine, a presentation, a manuscript, a brochure, or mailing of any type.

If your business offers the ability to receive and send information electronically, a setup that could save many clients hundreds or thousands of dollars or more each month in typesetting, courier, and disk transfer costs, and if you know what to do with all of it and how to make it look good and keep costs low, your small business immediately moves to the head of the line. Suddenly you will be the hottest thing in town. You are *modemhead.*

Clients will tell other people about the good deal they're getting and how much money they're saving. This is advertising you can't begin to pay for. It's called word of mouth, and it's what sells videos that are banned from MTV.

Secret #175   The secret world of computers after dark.

Did you ever wonder why you usually get busy signals if you call anyone at the office between 5:00 P.M. and 7:00 P.M. on a weekday?

It's because all the modem lines are using most of the telephones to send out that day's work electronically to service bureaus. The few remaining open lines are being used by the fax machines to send paper, or hard copies of the work produced on the computer, to the service bureaus so they can be used as proofs.

Not since Martha Mitchell blabbed during Watergate has so much information been flying through the telephone lines. Service bureaus are the nighttime dry cleaners and shirt laundries of the corporate world of information. In by 9 (P.M.), out by 6 (A.M.). They are the middle step in the production of material that businesses put out by the megatons every day. Service bureaus do magical things, such as transform IBM (and compatible) disks into MAC (and compatible) disks (or vice versa) for the modemless, print out color proofs for those of us who don't have $20,000 color printers, and produce pieces of film and high-resolution paper prints that will get printed in the form of reports, books, and magazines, which then are collated, distributed and/or mailed. Most service bureaus have several cost structures:

1. Regular service, which is delivery within 24 hours
2. Regular rush service, or 12–24 hours (cost is 50% higher)
3. Super duper rush service—two to 12 hours (100% more)

4. Next job status, which means they'll put your job on right after the one that's in there comes out (add 200% to the cost)

5. Pull job status, commonly used by lawyers and other important people in a hurry to get to court or lunch— the technician actually stops the work that's being processed and inserts the new job (for this you must pay five times the normal cost *and* give up your card to the health club)

6. David Copperfield Special, where they'll actually produce the work during creation, sometimes even before. Minimum cost on this is $25,000 per job and an invitation to a White House state dinner with Kevin Costner, Princess Diana, and the Ghost of Christmas Past.

This entire industry has sprung up as a result of the need to accommodate expanding computer capabilities, much to the growing chagrin of artists, printers, and professional typesetters who still produce artwork the old-fashioned way, cutting and pasting and setting everything by hand, hoping that the business world is suddenly going to see the light and revert back to how it used to be done.

Like we'd go back to black-and-white televisions and washing the clothes in the river.

Service bureaus have popped up everywhere, although the equipment is expensive (the type of linotronic printer required to produce work typically costs hundreds of thousands of dollars). Many print shops, typesetters, and what used to be called camera houses have recognized the trend and bought out existing bureaus, or added the equipment and knowledgeable people to their staff in order to be able to provide everything in-house; but many are independently owned.

With overnight, door-to-door courier service all across the continent and with your handy-dandy modem, any service bureau you want to use anywhere is as close as the next office.

I can't believe I wrote "handy-dandy."

Secret #176 There are some things you're too young to experience, even if you're 928 years old.

The main problem with the fax, modem, and other electronic marvels is this—you can achieve warp speed for days on end, and the client gets used to your super quick turnarounds, and you don't realize that you're zapping everything back and forth so fast that there's no room for error, much less incompetence. And suddenly you're in that state of constant hyperdrive. This you really have to be careful to avoid.

No kidding here. No wisecracks.

It can be a killer. At the very least, it can produce a profound sense of loss and depression after the rush period is over. This is not fun, and this is not why you decided to go into business for yourself.

Any time you feel it all closing in on you, go out and take a walk. Or a jog. Go shopping, or see a movie. To get your work done better, sometimes you have to get completely away from it. You'd be amazed how doing any one of these things can clear your mind and readjust your sense of balance.

Then you can tell the client who is pushing you so hard to finish his or her work to just go jump in the lake.

There. I've saved you $5,000 in doctor's bills and tests.

Secret #177 Move off, honey, I gotta do my report.

The Washington Post writes that the "hottest market of the '90s is between your knees and your navel," (2 April 1991) and they're not talking boxer shorts or bikini waxes.

They're talking laptop computers.

Don't confuse these with portables, which were about as handy as a loaded steamship trunk and had to be plugged in somewhere. The new laptops are battery-powered, light-weight, incredibly fast, and are becoming the item of choice to have on commuter buses and trains. And it's named for what it is—it sits on your lap.

Weighing in at a little less than a loaf of good Jewish rye bread, complete with keyboards, screens that use liquid crystal displays (LCDs), internal modems to connect to information sources at the office or wherever, and more memory capabilities than a lot of the older desktop computers, these things are utterly amazing, according to their users. People who need to take their work to the office or home, to business meetings in town or conferences across the country, or who don't want to waste the two-hour commute watching the guy across the aisle pick his nose swear these laptops are the best business tool since some enterprising Sumerian realized around 3300 B.C. that you could keep track of buying and selling by writing in symbols on clay tablets and changed commerce forever.

Prices for laptops are falling, and sales are going through the roof. Companies that analyze this information, such as Dataquest Inc., estimate that sales will increase at an annual rate of 44% through 1994, while sales of your basically boring desktop computers will grow only 4% a year.

So hey, what are you waiting for?

Oh wait—read the next secret before you rush out and buy your new toy.

Secret #178 Less is definitely better.

Forget PCs, forget portables, forget laptops. Notebooks are the wave of the future, according to people with their pulse on the future. (Just how do you take the future's pulse? I can't even find my own.) Notebook computers are about the size and shape of, well, a notebook. There are all types, and they can do just about anything that a computer can do, only faster.

Some you can type on, using a regular keyboard, and some you can scratch notes on, and while you're writing, it's translating your handwriting into—get this—*typed copy!*

So you want to be really careful if you're a doodler in meetings, because with their internal modems and ports for hooking up to printers and all types of network systems everywhere, the entire world could be sitting at their desks, watching you draw a handle bar mustache and horns on the photo of the woman holding this meeting, who is also chairperson of the board.

Plus every time you blink, they're improving these things with brighter display screens, greater memory, sliced black olives, and more functions being performed on fewer chips, which adds up to less weight, longer battery life, and extra cheese, which is what people really want.

Secret #179 You don't need to read this one if you can remember absolutely everything you have ever done.

You are working in your office when suddenly, you hear the smoke alarm go off! Fire engines screech to a halt in front. A megaphone is ordering you and everyone inside with you to leave the building immediately. Possessed with an amazing sense of calm, you realize you only have time to grab one thing. What's it going to be—your bag? Coat? Family photos?

Think again.

If you want to recover quickly and get your business back on its feet, grab your computer work disks.

You've spent months, maybe years, doing all this work. Where would your business be without these records? Could you remember all that you need to remember to re-create your records and start up again? Insurance can cover the loss of your equipment but, as far as I've ever heard, not the value of the software you've created.

Protecting your disks should become an obsession. I know you know this, but it can't hurt to remind you: make backup copies of your work every day and leave the backups in a different place from where you store your disks, if possible. Many people take their backup work home, or keep it in another place at night, in case something happens at the office.

IMPORTANT NOTE: Always be careful about where you put your disks. If you ride a subway train to and from work, for instance, and you're carrying your disks with you, *do not* put the disks on the floor of the train car unless you want to have everything erased. Keep your disks far away from magnets or anything with an electromagnetic field. When you put a disk near a magnet, it tends to forget all it ever knew, like everyone connected with the Iran-Contra affair.

Secret #180 Everybody's shooting
in the dark.

If you tack a key word such as "Incorporated" or "Consulting" on your business card and act as though you know what you're doing after you turn on your computer, you begin to acquire a reputation. Clients, suppliers, and other people who have the same word-processing, design, or spreadsheet programs as you do will start to bombard you with questions. They can't get their equipment to do something, or they don't know why the program won't work, or why their printer is acting like this.

You can pretty much look like a complete genius by telling people to try one of these three things:

1. Check the cables. In the back of the hard drive, there is a panel with all sorts of hookups and ports and squigits that look important. A printer, for instance, hooks into its own port, and a monitor and modem each get one. Every item that is connected to the computer has a certain place it's gotta be, or it won't work. When someone has upgraded to a new piece of equipment, or some brilliant waste of space has had all the desks and computers moved around, chances are that a cable isn't hooked up right, or that it isn't firmly in place.

2. Find the "Help" screen for software problems. Inside each computer ever built, there are little tiny helpful people who look like your sweet Aunt Dottie, and who bake little tiny nanosecond cookies and just really want to help you.

If you don't buy that, then believe this—just about every program has a way to get into the help screen. Figuring out how might take all the bytes out of your bits, but you could maybe check the manual, if all else fails.

Macintosh usually has something up on the menu line at the top of the screen that gets you to a place where you can ask for help.

With IBM-types, you can push ALT-Z or maybe ALT-H or CTRL-H or F10 or F3. There is a whiff of a rumor that these DOS-type animals are trying to standardize the F1 function key as a help key.

But hey, don't do it on *our* account, right?

3. Turn the printer (or modem or hard drive or whatever) off, wait a few minutes, then turn it back on. This one is so simple, it kills me. When Kathy installed a new program, she had to type in some instructions to the printer. For some never-to-be-known reason, the printer did not respond. We begged, we pleaded, we bribed. Nothing worked. Then she walked around to the back of the printer and shut it off.

After a few minutes, she turned it back on, and it did exactly what she told it to do.

Why?

It's magic, is why.

The scientific explanation, which someone at a computer store told us later, is that this simple act clears the printer's memory, and if there happened to be a stray command inside there that was screwing up the works, it just got zapped.

I think I'll stick with the magic thing.

Secret #181 Take good care of yourself.

If you work with a computer, please consider these tips on how to prevent injuries and strains. They're from an orthopedic surgeon, also called an orthopod, which sounds like something you'd find on your tomato plants:

1. Get the right chair. Not just the extra dining room chair. A good chair is going to accommodate you or your huge Uncle Bert; it's going to be adjustable in height, at the armrests, and at the back.

   If you sit most or all of the time, check out the chairs designed to put your weight on your knees and legs rather than at the base of your spine. They're not cheap—you could buy a used car for less money, and they look funny, but so do you if you're not able to sit or walk without pain because you've injured your back.

   Whatever type you get, ergonomics experts say to support your lower back by putting your feet on the floor or a footstool. The ideal is to have your hips at 90 degrees to your torso.

   Marvin Dainoff, director of the Center for Ergonomic Research at Miami University, recommends that you sit up straight and not slump forward. ''It feels good temporarily, but things I've read suggest that if you do it long enough—for months, years—there's some danger to your discs.'' He also advises not to stay in the same position for long periods of time, which leads us to the next pointer of the day:

2. Stand up and stretch or move around every hour or so. This is so your skeletal mass doesn't turn into a

fossil. It's good to get up, it refreshes you, it will make you look like a movie star who does commercials for a health spa. Hey, I'll say anything to get you out of that position for a few minutes. Give your bod a break.

3. Place your work at eye level, on both sides of the screen. Get two of those holders for your work that attach to the sides of your terminal, and mount them at eye level, one on the left, one on the right. Use the left side one week, then the right side the next week. This way you won't get the world's worst crick in your neck, plus you won't establish patterns that can create a severe injury.

4. Don't leave heavy manuals, magazines, and other stuff that you use and refer to down near the floor. Every time you lean over to pick up one of these monsters, you're possibly reinforcing a weakness in your muscles, which can lead to some serious problems. Put the ones you use the most on shelves next to you at waist level or above. Jeepers, you'd think I wouldn't have to tell you this.

5. Position your computer so the rays don't hit anyone valuable, such as yourself. There's a lot of discussion going on about electromagnetic fields (EMFs) produced by computer monitors, or video display terminals (VDTs), in the places where you and I work (PWYAIWs) and the possible problems associated with these EMFs, such as miscarriages, green eyebrows, and extraordinarily large right feet. The National Institute for Occupational Safety and Health (NIOSH) released a report in March 1991, concluding that "the use of VDTs and exposure to the electromagnetic fields they produce were not associated with an increased risk of spontaneous abortion." They said absolutely nothing about the green eyebrows and right feet.

Some manufacturers swear that there is no problem,

and even advertise this, but the fact is that there have not been any major experiments in the United States to investigate the biologic effects of VDT emissions (*The Washington Post,* 18 March 1991). The Computer and Business Equipment Manufacturers Association claims that there is no danger to humans, but they welcome studies and more answers. Sure, like the Third World welcomes cholera.

What seems to have more people worried now is extremely low frequency (ELF) fields, which come not only from computer terminals, but also from your toaster, coffee maker, television, and other electrical appliances, as well as from wiring and power lines.

Here's something to help you make up your mind about whether or not to keep your face at least 12 inches away from the terminal. The staff of the computer magazine *MacWorld* isn't satisfied that everything is all hunky-dory, so they have redesigned their cubicle offices to avoid having people sitting right in back of someone else's terminal, where the rays are more powerful; they all keep that minimum 12-inch distance from the front of the screen, as well.

NOTE: Some people, such as Kathy, my business partner, actually prefer to stand while they work at the computer. She has the monitor mounted at eye level for her, which means I stand on a ladder to work at her computer, but no problem. This is probably better for your circulation and posture, although you'll note that nobody scientific is quoted here. It's certainly better for Kathy, who enjoys the freedom of movement she has by standing.

A few words from our Please Don't Let Computer Terms Ruin Our Elegant Language department:

These are nouns:

Access (can be an adjective, such as access code, or access charge; some well-meaning people have actually forced it to double as a verb)

Fax, or *Facsimile* (this word, too, has been used as a verb, believe it or not)

Impact (they've also made it into a verb)

Input/Output (strictly for computers, but some people have been known to use these words for humans and other things, as well as turn them into verbs)

Interface (you're not going to believe this, but some people use this as a verb, also)

Modem (you don't modem anything to anyone; you send it by modem, but again, some people have been known to make it into a verb)

The Care and Feeding of the Common (and Not-So-Common) Client

Secret #182   Crème de la crème.

Some clients know what buttons to push to get you to want to do your best work.

If you're lucky enough to have a client like this, you know what I mean.

For these people, you'll rearrange billings, you'll push some work through and not charge them for your time, you'll meet deadlines that were impossible to begin with, you'll work harder than you should, and you won't mind any of it too much, unless something comes up to make you miss your niece's piano recital. Which, if the client knows about it, she or he won't let you miss, either.

That's the main difference between these certain clients and everyone else out there—they respect that you have a life and that you want to hear a niece who could be playing at the elementary school or at Carnegie Hall. They respect your skills, your professionalism, your advice, your attitude, and your willingness to work as one of their staff or team members, but they never forget that you're not.

To find clients like this, all you have to do is be incredibly lucky.

Secret #183 If the boss says she/he wants to see you right after lunch, take a long lunch.

Sometimes the weirdest things happen.

Around 2:26 P.M. one afternoon, a client called. We had been working with this man for several years, and his company had grown into our biggest account. However, due to budget cutbacks and other factors, this account had not exactly been a ton of fun recently, and we had sensed those little electric zings of warning.

He, along with several other people in middle and top management, had just been fired, and he wanted to tell us goodbye. He also said that this probably meant the end of our relationship with this company, although it was certainly not the end of our friendship.

My first reaction was no reaction, then about a half-second of panic, followed by an odd kind of relief. After 12 years and many, many corporate sweeps like this, you begin to sense when something bad is looming behind lunch. People always get fired after lunch, did you ever notice?

I congratulated him and wished him well in his new life. When I told Kathy, she and I talked about how this freed us up to go after some other types of accounts that we'd had no time to pursue lately, such as more illustration and writing work. I began to make a list of places to start calling the next day.

Now here's the weird part:

That same afternoon, we received a call from an editor with a large association who wanted us to bring in our portfolio sometime that week. His boss was interested in talking with us about doing some work for them, some brochures, a few booklets, and oh yes—they had a monthly magazine that they wanted to talk about having redesigned and handled. It would be a lot of work, and they were looking at various design studios around town. Were we interested?

Were we interested?

The fact that this call came in at this time was amazing. It usually takes weeks or months of work to get a solid lead like this.

Call it a coincidence, call it luck, call it fate or part of the plan. I honestly don't know what it is, but whatever it is, it's wonderful.

Secret #184   I just realized what it is. It's the RDF.

There was one other thing at work here, and that was the Rick Dobson Factor (RDF).

You can't buy or bribe anyone to get an RDF. The only way to have it on your side is to actually know a guy named Rick Dobson who is decent and fair and work with him for several years and prove to him that you can do anything at all, creatively and beautifully, at a reasonable price, and then Rick recommends you to people who call him and ask, "Hey, Rick, do you know who we could call to do a good job for us on this project and keep the budget down on this planet?"

And the next thing you know, total strangers are calling you, asking you to come over and talk about wonderful work that they want you to do, and they say they got your name from a man who got it from Rick Dobson.

P.S. If you don't know a guy named Rick Dobson, you can have a (your client's name here) Factor of your own. The important thing is that he or she be a mensch, and that you be willing to work your complete butt off.

Secret #185 Hope for the best, but prepare for the worst.

Our appointment with Mr. Graham was at 10:00 A.M. We arrived at 9:45 A.M.

Brochures, booklets, folders, inserts, and other material we can handle with no sweat—we've been doing stuff like this for years, and we can save our clients all sorts of money by designing and producing them on the computer.

But a magazine, rich and full of creative promise, 50 or 60 editorial pages plus a cover just waiting to be redesigned and produced brand new each month, this was the Empire State Building to us. No—make that K-2. And we were jumping up and down on one foot for the chance to prove we could climb it.

We presented our cost proposal which, although carefully thought out, was a total stab in the dark, money-wise. We had no idea how much time would be involved.

And then Mr. Graham, the president of the association, had some questions for us.

Had we ever done a magazine before?

Uh, no, actually, we had not, but we . . .

Had we ever designed any magazine pages before?

Well, plenty of ads, yes, but no editorial.

How about the cover—had we ever designed a cover?

Yes, as a matter of fact, Kathy had done an illustrated cover for a client, sort of a takeoff on *Time*, which had been used as an insert in that same magazine.

But it wasn't the real cover?

No, but it could have been.

Hmmm-m-m-m-m.

Mr. Graham said that he was talking with several other design studios that specialized in magazines, and that he would get back to us in a few weeks.

We were eager to do the work, and we were brimming with hope. But we were also realists.

We started looking for other new accounts.

Secret #186 There seems to be a pattern here.

We landed the magazine account. We were thrilled!

We guessed that the reasons we got it were because we were enthusiastic about it, though not exactly experienced in magazines, and that they liked what they had seen of our other work.

What we didn't know until later was that we got it precisely because of our lack of experience, in addition to the other reasons.

A few weeks before reaching his final decision, Mr. Graham had been waiting in the lobby of a place that specialized in magazine design, where framed copies of a dozen or so different magazines were hanging on the walls. He realized something that the designers had no intention of showing: all the magazines looked alike.

He did not want his magazine to look like all these others.

He wanted something fresh and original, something hot, something different.

And he knew exactly who would work the hardest to pull it off.

We got the account.

Secret #187 Guess who's coming to celebrate.

It had been a long, hot summer, the one after we landed the magazine account. We had worked harder than we thought we could, lost 10 pounds each, and Kathy had aggravated a slipped disk by sitting at the computer for 12-hour days earlier in the summer. She had been told by her doctor to either stand or lie down, but she was not supposed to sit. So the monitor was up on the dining room chair, which was placed on top of her desk, and she was standing while she worked, and she liked it so much that she'd decided to make it a permanent arrangement.

The office looked as fabulous as you would expect.

Heaps and heaps of piles of stacks of boxes of work were everywhere, on every surface throughout the office and the entire house. We had not had time to clean the place or open the mail or cook anything more complicated than tomato soup in weeks. TV dinners were stuck to the walls (well, not really, but you get the picture). Pantyhose were tossed over the couch. Dustballs so big you could hop on them and ride away into the sunset were in the corners.

But we had managed to get all the work out, on time, and our clients were pleased.

We were talking about how nice it would be to take our clients out to lunch at a restaurant downtown, maybe celebrate when the printed magazine was delivered, which would be any day now.

Now remember what a mess our place is. Okay.

Knock, knock. (At our front door.)

Who's there?

Ken and Larry.

Ken and Larry who?

Ken and Larry our magazine guys, that's who!

Kathy opened the door to see the president of the association, Larry Graham, and the editor, Ken Koepper, holding the first copies off the presses and a bottle of very nice champagne.

Up until that moment, the president had no idea that we worked out of our home. It just never came up, and we don't go around blabbing about it or scribbling it on restroom walls or anything. Over the years, we have always made it a point to go to our clients' offices for meetings, or to meet them at a convenient restaurant for lunch. No one had ever dropped in uninvited like this.

To their great credit, they acted as though they hardly noticed. (Maybe it wasn't an act. Maybe they really didn't notice the appalling mess.) The chaos did not seem to matter to them in the least. There was a lot of pride in how great the magazine looked, and the popping of the champagne cork, and a couple of toasts to a long and healthy working relationship, and then they left.

What I learned that day was that anyone with whom you work can drop by at any time for any reason, and it's cool to be somewhat prepared for that to happen so they don't think your idea of housekeeping was formed in Dogpatch.

I also learned that clients appreciate it when you are giving them the best you've got.

Secret #188 Fifty ways to love your liver (and keep your account).

No matter what most clients say or do, they really won't trust you if you've had too much booze or other hard drugs. Showing a weakness here can take you down faster than a Grand Hyatt express elevator.

One big reason is that you probably know too much—like who's going to get fired next week and all sorts of other things about their business, and that their kid was arrested, and other intimate details about their lives—and if you start blabbing while under the influence, they're dead meat. Another huge reason is that if they know you can lose control around them, they know you can lose control around others, including their competitors. This is not what you want your client thinking about you.

Only you know your limits in this area. Show your best professional judgment about drugs. The longer you have a working relationship, the more important it is to work at this, if you want to keep their trust. Every luncheon and working dinner, every meeting and conference, every time you deal with your client for any reason, even if it's a clandestine rendezvous, don't go over the edge with booze or drugs. It's a thin line, and nobody's gotta walk it.

Secret #189 To anyone who is having an affair with a client.

Speaking of the clandestine rendezvous, whether or not you are carrying on an affair with your client is no one's business but yours and your lover's. This may be about as safe for your business as skydiving without a parachute, but who knows—you might like working at Burgers R Us after you lose it all.

And that's absolutely *all* I'm going to say about this.

(You are looking at blank space.)

(You are still looking at blank space.)

Secret #190 Act as though you never have any problems.

Some clients seem to enjoy a few minutes of chitchat, others don't even bother to say hello or ask you if you have a minute before they launch into their crisis of the moment. But there is one thing all clients have in common—they *hate* to hear about your problems.

Remember that clients actually have to work in offices like you used to work in, where they face political battles, angry bosses, power struggles, smelly coworkers, and other types of threatening situations.

And this is all before the first coffee break.

To the average client, it doesn't really matter whether you have a hangnail or have just been released from being held hostage for 27 hours by People for More Sugar on Frosted Flakes. All the client wants to know is if you can send a hot rush courier over with a draft of his or her latest job, and by the way, the chairman or legal department wants to take a quick look at it, which means that it's going to completely change, and you're going to be up all night making those changes.

To the client, you don't have any problems.

How you look to the client:	*How it really is:*
You are the boss.	You have all the worries.
You are a free person.	You haven't had a day off in 10 years.

How you look to the client:	*How it really is:*
You send his or her company invoices for thousands of dollars, of which you could pocket every penny and go off to New Zealand on extended backpacking trips	Every cent of every check has to go toward expenses, and you're lucky if you can cover a monthly salary for yourself.
You have music in the background, you sound cheerful, therefore your life is perfect.	Ever since your hi-fi broke down in 1972, you've had to make do with a transistor radio that you found in the trash.
You are doing exactly what they want to be doing.	You are doing exactly what you want to be doing.

Don't poke a hole in your client's bubble. Listening in on your life is as close as many people are ever going to get to running a business. At least let them imagine how great it must be for you. Always answer every, How are you? with Fine! or Great! Most clients don't care to find out how you really are.

For those who do care, they usually don't have the time to listen to anything.

If you have a client who both cares and has time, you have your mother on the phone.

Secret #191 Will popcorn be served?

We used to work with a client who had one priority above all others: FIRST PIN BLAME.

You know I just love an attitude like this.

It didn't matter what was going on, or how quickly we might need to act in order to change something. The only thing that seemed to matter was *whose fault is this?*

He would spend hours sifting through his early notes, trying to find out exactly when this happened and who said what, determining who was going to pay for it.

One of the most memorable adventures involved a printer who used a different color of ink from the one that Kathy picked. Now this is not exactly the type of thing that you'd get in the mail and look at and think right away, AHA! wrong color! The client thought we should have stood over the presses while it was being printed. Most clients would have blamed the printer and dropped it. His action was to blame us for it and take a big chunk off of our fee.

More than once, we lost invaluable time because we had to go to his office for an emergency meeting so that he could get to the bottom of something. He did eventually get to the bottom of something—our patience. We resigned the account.

It would be nice if I could write that once you've been through this, you know how to handle it. But I don't think that's true. Paranoid clients are kind of like the creature in *Alien*. There's no way to know what form their paranoia will take or where it will pop out next.

Plus the creature was a lot cuter.

Secret #192 Who's been sitting in my chair?

Ah, the great American corporate meeting. I really hate most of these sessions.

People line up around a huge rectangular wooden conference table, somberly taking the same chairs they usually take, somberly placing their notebooks and pens down at their spot before somberly going off to get coffee, and then somberly falling asleep mentally during the entire meeting, which lasts for the rest of your life.

We had one client who had moved to new offices. In the conference room was something completely different—a huge oval table, with the center cut out. For some reason, I noticed that the president fidgeted during the entire meeting, waffling about jobs and deadlines, looking over in my direction as though I were sitting on his nest or something. I had no idea what his problem was until someone told me later I had been in *His Chair.*

Well, how do you know what's the head of the table with a shape like this?

I now walk into meetings last and take whatever chair is available.

Secret #193 Looking for Mr./Ms. Right.

There are certain qualities and traits that you might want to look for in a client with whom you would like to establish a long-term relationship. Here are a few from my list.

1. **Must have sense of humor.** This doesn't mean you get a bucket of water splashed on your head when you walk into someone's office, or joke questions about your contagious leprosy in a crowded elevator. You want to find someone who can laugh at himself or herself, as well as situations. Someone who knows the difference between meetings and funerals. Actually, I've been to funerals that were more fun than many client meetings. One time, this two year old kid got into the organ room . . .

2. **Should be honest with you.** If they have a problem with your work, your billings, your attitude, your nail polish, your anything, they should tell you, not their staff people, not the night janitor, not your other clients.

3. **Being human would help.** Not every person is human, as you probably already know. There are people who never make mistakes, who never have to go to the bathroom, who are so perfect that they make you feel as though you're in an eggshell art museum the moment you step into their office. Give me a guy who spills coffee across his desk while reaching to shake my hand and who doesn't let it ruin his or my entire life. That's my kind of client.

4. **Trusts your judgment.** You want to occasionally hear comments like, "You should decide that," or

''I'm going to leave that up to you,'' and this is in addition to what to order from the deli to be delivered for lunch.

5. **Doesn't bug you any more than necessary.** Some clients think that just because the work is off their desk or out of their computer, they should see proofs or drafts immediately. As if it just springs into being. They forget about the time needed to actually do the work. Some can even bug you so much for anticipated delivery dates, as well as to begin scheduling new projects, that you don't have time to do the work.

6. **Processes your bills promptly.** Any person running a small business should get paid within 15 to 20 days, and most clients are capable of making this happen. Accounting departments are the most efficient places in the universe when it's time to send out bills, and believe it or not, they're the same departments that issue checks to people like you and me. Insist that your bills be paid on time, and give a small discount for prompt payment, if you think it will help or if you really like the client. But don't let the client think you can wait 42 or 60 days for your money. If you had wanted to be in the banking business, you would have opened a bank.

7. **Occasionally tells you the finished project looks good.** Or at least mentions once a year that your work is appreciated. This is a nice touch. You can live without it, but like a box of Godiva chocolates on St. Valentine's Day, it's one of those small luxuries that makes you feel good.

8. **Actually sends you Godiva chocolates.** You've got one in a skillion, if you have this.

9. **Tells other potential clients about you.** (Remember the RDF.) This says far more than that they like your work. This, in fact, is priceless.

It's Just Good
Management

Secret #194 What is all this stuff?

Look around you. Within arm's reach of your chair, or certainly within the radius that you roll around in on your chair, there is an average of 35 to 42 hours of paperwork that you have put off doing for months, maybe years. Time management consultants know this, and they know how long it's been since you clipped your toenails, too. They say that the average time we have each week to do this is 10 hours. I think they mean the paperwork, not the clipping of toenails.

Getting organized is near the top of every busy person's list, but most of us running a small business can't take the time from our schedule to actually do it.

Organizational experts say that if you're the type of person who is really bothered by this, it can cost you big time since you feel a constant sense of dread due to the overwhelming loss of control over your life.

On the other hand, psychologists say that for some people, being disorganized is what makes them tick, that disorganization is an attention-getter, or an excuse for putting off the work they absolutely hate to do, or a way to avoid responsibility. (Well, I certainly didn't see *that* letter.)

The secret is to figure out whether you like walnuts or pecans in your brownie. Then you have some basis to go on here, because as we all know, brownie consumption is critical to effective thinking about life and work and junk.

There are organizers who make a full-time career of, and who you can bet are kept in complete stitches by, sorting through the stacks and heaps and boxes and cabinets of paperwork accumulated by businesses of all sizes. Imagine what they must see before lunch.

All of these people agree on one thing: handle every piece of paper only one time.

Stephanie Winston, founder of the Organizing Principle in Manhattan, as well as author of *The Organized Executive,* recommends you do one of four things with a piece of paper that you come in contact with:

1. Toss it
2. Refer it
3. Act on it
4. File it

She calls it her TRAF system, which immediately leaps out to me as meaning TRAFFIC ADJUDICATION, which reminds me that I forgot to pay a parking ticket that I put into my "Act on it" file about two years ago.

Stephanie Culp suggests in her book, *How to Conquer Clutter,* that you can set up five labeled baskets:

1. To do
2. To pay
3. To file
4. To read
5. To trash

The first two should be placed on your desk so you can act on them, the third one can be kept underneath your desk, and the fourth one kept close by your desk so you can take stuff out of it to wherever you take stuff you read. She also recommends bagging a Pending basket since paper can hang out there until the next ice age.

I would like to add my key recommendation here that someone with a first name besides Stephanie write a book about organization.

Secret #195 No, we don't want the business credit card, or the polka-dot fax paper, and by the way, how did our company get on so many mailing lists?

During your first year or two in business for yourself, you may be in a state of awe about everything. That this is happening at all is miraculous. People actually call you to do work for them. Wow! And they pay!

After around the fourth or fifth year of running your small business, you may reach a plateau. Things aren't so fresh and new anymore. For one thing, it seems as though the mail now gets delivered by tractor-trailer truck. You're on every junk list in the world, and you find yourself opening only checks, bills, and letters from people you really like, and tossing everything else into a big box to open later. Twenty strong huskies couldn't pull that box by now.

Some people develop an attitude (is this really what I want to do professionally?), some find they can't stop worrying about money/taxes, some of us can't sleep so well, and some people just get bored. Projects that once looked exciting now seem like chores. All the hassles that you endured in those early years—why do you still have them? Isn't success supposed to be smoother than this, you may start to wonder. And, by the way, you can also begin to wonder, why aren't I successful, as in rich?

Why am I still working so hard, for not nearly enough money? Why do I still have to prove myself to every new account? Why do I even have to go find new accounts? You may even find yourself hoping—against all odds—that just *once* the IRS would say you don't have to file your 941 or pay FICA, just for *one month*, for crying out loud.

You feel as though no one else could ever possibly understand what you're going through.

You have lost control of your set.

You are now entering the twilight zone.

Secret #196 You are now leaving the twilight zone. (See, that wasn't so bad, was it?)

If your business is older than five years, you are one of the survivors. You have crossed the mountains. And just look at all those notches on your belt.

You're much more confident now. You've probably had the chance to say no to a project or work you did not want, or more likely, to people with whom you did not want to work.

You're stronger, having lived through the explosive boom times, the recession that no one admitted to, and the depression that seems to underlie everything.

You've supported yourself for all these years by doing what you want to do. Even if your company earned only $100 last year, this was more profit than the federal government and most of the 50 states showed on their balance sheets, as well as major film studios, auto manufacturers, airlines, and other companies that ended up in the red. And we won't even talk about banks or S&Ls.

Your track record is pretty good, if not amazing.

You finally have a good accountant.

Your company has been recommended by others.

You've probably won a few awards or kudos.

Your clients say thank you once a year.

You manage to keep your good humor and quiet grace. (Well, okay, that may be stretching it for some people. But your nieces and nephews think you're darned funny.)

And before you know it, you're going to start receiving

10-year-anniversary mail. You won't believe the junk you'll get after being in business for 10 years.

People will want you to buy everything. Pens that say your company name, with "10 Year Anniversary" written out. Gold-foil engraved stickers to put at the top of your letterhead. Paperweights and hats. Who could possibly think that we'd want to buy any of those baseball hats that guys wear backwards while driving their pickup trucks in Missouri and Arkansas?

Actually, they might be cute to wear the next time you meet a client for lunch.

Secret #197 Point of no return.

Okay, you've crossed the plateau, entered and exited the twilight zone, scaled the mountains, and completely proven the Small Business Administration was wrong by defying those horrible odds that they give for success.

You have hung on for several years, maybe even a decade.

You might have established such a good reputation that people are offering you jobs, or other companies are asking if they can buy you out.

This may be the ultimate compliment, but you're not interested. (Well, if you are so flattered and flatulent you can't stand yourself, why the %&*()$#@! are you reading this book about running your own business?)

This is what you'll discover—after you've run your business for this long, you're going to find it's impossible to go back to a regular-type job. Just the thought of having to get up at 5:30 A.M. again (you may stumble out of bed this early now, but it's not because you have to), or working out which form of transportation to take, or having to decide what to wear every day, or facing the politics of it all is going to make you feel nauseated.

It's like keeping the cat inside once she's seen Paris. Or your backyard.

Secret #198 Does anybody have a Tums?

Getting away from work can be harder than getting the work in the first place. Some clients are decent about it, and some will act as though their children will starve if you take off one day or an afternoon. But after a long time with no breaks, your body and mind start to give you warning signs that you must listen to and act on, subtle things such as:

- An uncontrollable reaction to a ringing phone, which is to point your hands at it and pretend like you're shooting it with an automatic weapon, complete with the spitty gunshot noises that you perfected in the sixth grade;

- Finding yourself in the fetal position on the floor, counting cat hairs in the carpet, with no clear memory of how long you've been there, and no good reason to get up just yet;

- Sharp gas pains that you've had in your lower chest/stomach area since Sunday night; you suddenly are seized with the horrific thought that you are experiencing cardiac arrest, except you realize it's probably the brussels sprouts and cauliflower;

- Frequently answering someone's casual "How's it going" with a comment such as "terrible," or "unbelievably awful," or "terribly, unbelievably, indescribably awful" and going into detail about what is so horrible in your life now—as if anyone, *especially* a client, wants to hear this;

- Not noticing that spring has burst out of every bud and

plant and tree, or that the month-long heat wave broke and it is now under 90°F, or that there is a rainbow beginning in your yard.

The whole idea behind being the boss is that you can manage your time and yourself better. True, you can't control outside factors, but you can control how you react to them, for the most part.

By deciding when to answer the phone, and when to let the service pick up for you while you watch Rocky & Bullwinkle cartoons away from the sound and fury of the phones, by determining what jobs can wait so you can sit out in the back or on the balcony for an hour and look at nothing while you collect your thoughts, you are taking charge again.

It works. You come back refreshed, ready to tackle anything that needs to be done. If it doesn't matter much to you that you deserve it, at least consider that this is what your clients deserve.

Secret #199   What do you mean, you want to be off work the Friday after Thanksgiving?

You can't expect that anyone else should care as much as you do about the success of your business. Why should they? It's your business, not theirs. Did you ever care about another one as much as you do your own? Many people figure that if they're going to put their soul into anything, it's going to be their own company. Does that feeling sound vaguely familiar?

So how far should you push other people to do work for you beyond the normal hours?

My opinion is you shouldn't push at all. The people you have carefully selected to work with you should be so inspired by your compassion and passion, by your dedication to their success as well as your own, that they will do extraordinary things for you without even being asked.

Well, with any luck, they'll at least show up on time and do the work they're supposed to do.

Always remember that just about everybody has somebody who needs them. People have to get to a daughter's little league game, or take a son to ballet lessons, or occasionally wait at home for the roofer, painter, or plumber to show up. Everyone has a life outside of your company.

If you have to ask for overtime help or weekend work, make sure it's terribly important. Then do it yourself, if possible.

And come on—you can give them the day after Thanksgiving, as well as the day after Christmas. With pay.

Secret #200 Here's coming at you, kid.

It is reasonable to expect some things from an employee, and most of these are straight out of the cornball, old-fashioned department. I believe that if you give them, you'll get them back, in most cases. (But then I also believe that it's possible to feed everyone in the world.)

1. A sense of honor. (Like if the computer has produced a paycheck with 12 more digits than it should have, he/she could mention it to you.)

2. Loyalty. (You should hear juicy stuff first, before everyone else in the office does.)

3. Discretion in all areas. (Particularly in the area of client projects and billings. No information should ever be blabbed to anyone outside the office about *any* work done for your clients. This can cause your company to lose accounts, plus it's just plain wrong.)

4. Honesty.

5. One original thought or idea per year. (Optional. This is a lot for some people.)

6. Perhaps a birthday card for you from everyone. (Also optional. Depends on how you feel about your birthday, and whether or not you've given employees something small on their birthdays, such as the day off.)

7. A sense of humor, or at least an occasional laugh at one of your jokes.

Secret #201 Would you care for one of these nice little cockroach puffs, or perhaps you'd like to step into our stockade?

We toured a house where a woman had been running a design studio in her basement for several years. She was in the process of moving her operation over to a storefront nearby, and she was trying to rent her house. Kathy had been curious to see if maybe this other house had more office space, and I had been just plain curious.

The woman had four artists on her staff. We noticed that each artist's table was placed facing a concrete block wall that had no windows.

Kathy asked if this was a good arrangement for the artists, if this gave them more room to work. The woman's reply was that this was a good setup for her business, that when the tables had faced each other, the artists had talked more among themselves and had not gotten their work done as quickly. Placing the tables up against the wall deterred conversation, and she could get more work out of them.

Wow, do I love this attitude.

Why not bring in rats and roaches to complete the dungeon effect? Maybe a nice stockade over in the corner.

Don't do this to people who work with you, okay? I'll have to put you in my next book, if you do.

I don't mean to suggest that you need to be some kind of Perle Mesta or The World's Greatest Hostess or Host when people come to work with you, but there is a happy medium somewhere. Although mediums, I understand, are tortured people and do not enjoy many aspects of their work, particularly when they have to connect you to dead people so you can ask where they buried their treasures or left the latest will or whatever.

Secret #202 A good person is hard to find.

You are probably going to need help occasionally, whether it's just to have someone come in and check your mail while you're off on one of those frequent trips around the world that small business owners take at the drop of a hat, or to have someone take your place when you leave.

Ideally, your partner can help. Even though you may not do the same job function, you both deal with the same clients and can overlap and help out in critical areas.

If you're in this alone, however, or even if you have a partner, you may realize at some point that it would be nice to have help on a small project basis. Especially if you are bogged down with enough detail work to fill in the Grand Canyon.

Finding someone you can trust to do the work right and represent you well to your client is definitely not the easiest thing you're going to come up against. You may get lucky; you may run an ad that will turn up someone great, or find the perfect person through an employment agency, or talk with another professional who recommends someone to you.

A good place to start looking for outside help is to dig up people with whom you used to work and whom you trust.

I met Susan Hankoff Estrella when she and I worked together in the creative department at the ad agency that fired me, thanks again. She has proven to be the best thing that has ever happened to us, freelance professionally-wise speaking.

Susan, a very talented artist, is almost completely self-taught about designing and producing artwork on the Macintosh computer. She and Kathy think alike much of the time. Susan has proven to be a tremendous asset to the smooth operation of our business.

Sometimes the people who help your business turn out to be related to you. As long as you pay them on a professional basis, and they want and know how to do the work, there is no better source of help, I'm convinced. If your family lives far away, as mine does, the idea of asking them to help out is not an option. And for some of you, the whole concept of paying family members might not be the best idea you've ever heard. But you know your family, and if it clicks, lucky you.

There are plenty of other ways to find dedicated people to help out—look around you. Whom do you trust? Is there an elderly man who walks around the neighborhood, stops to chat, asks about your business? Is there a young, energetic mother who would like to reorganize your supply closet or storage area while her kids are in school? Ask your local merchants; check bulletin boards to see who is looking for what, or put up a job description with your phone number.

Sometimes neighbors and close friends are practically dying for a chance to come in and help you by doing things such as covering the telephones, doing mailings, entering data for you, delivering baskets or packages or whatever you need delivered. They would be thrilled if you asked them to help. All people, and particularly the oldest and the youngest ones, love to feel needed and trusted.

Good people are out there. You just have to give them a chance.

Secret #203 Everybody's got
problems.

Here are just a few of the reasons that you may hear for
why someone has to miss work:

The car wouldn't start.

I got rear-ended on the way in.

Traffic was unbelievable!

We want to get an early start for the weekend.

My hair looks like Godzilla and the only appointment I
can get is at 10:00 A.M. tomorrow.

I gotta see my kid's teacher or counselor.

My entire family is flying in early for the wedding.

The plumber is coming, but I don't know what time.

The bedroom furniture is being delivered, but I don't
know what time.

The air conditioning is on the fritz, and they're coming
tomorrow, but I don't know what time.

The furnace blew up (you fill in the rest).

These are all part of what we call "life," and your business has to be flexible enough to put up with some of it.

All people have personal problems, health problems, sick
kids, doctor's appointments. They may ask for flexible
hours, want to share their job with someone else, want to
get more help, take on more work, take training courses in
a place like San Diego, be worth more to you so they can
have a raise. They are ambitious, infuriating, dedicated, for-
getful, and loyal.

Sometimes they have to be praised, or chewed out, or
put on notice. And sometimes they have to be fired. (*Yikes!*
Do you have to let someone go? See the following two
secrets.)

You will find yourself in the position of being mother

superior, father confessor, big sister or big brother, under-standing parent, banker, wonderful employer, and horrible person. All in the same day.

It's all part of running a business. They may be people with problems, but at least they're your people.

Secret #204 Here's one of those phrases you will never hear—"You can't fire me because I QUIT!"

This phrase went out with other oldies such as "Put the kibosh on it" and "I'll have one more for the road." Nobody quits anymore instead of being fired, except maybe the president of the United States.

If a person quits, he or she won't get unemployment insurance. Sometimes unemployment insurance is the only thing standing between him or her and cat food for dinner, since most people are not independently wealthy.

To be fair, put this person on notice that he or she is not pulling enough weight and that you expect more effort, or that your business is in trouble, or that things are about to change for whatever reason. Then it won't come as a total shock.

Having been fired once myself, I know from experience that above all, it's embarrassing for both parties. We all want to be popular and well liked, and getting fired does nothing for your self-esteem in these areas.

If you have to do it, do it with the skill of a surgeon, quickly, quietly, cleanly. Wait until about an hour or two before the end of the working day, giving them enough time to collect their things and say goodbye to some people. Explain the true reason, and have a box of Kleenex tissues on hand. Give as much severance pay as your company can afford, at least three or four weeks of pay. Your company is going to be better off, so you can put a little humanity into this, even if you have to borrow it.

Be willing to give the person an honest written reference about their abilities, but chances are he or she won't ask you for one if they have not felt good about their work.

Don't let your guilt cause you to try to be friends with this person afterwards (unless you are already friends). The best way you can help is to wish them good luck and say goodbye.

Oh, and one more very important thing—read the next secret.

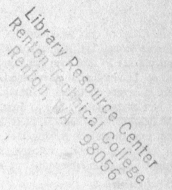

Secret #205 Safeguard your company's work from that one person who will try to destroy it.

A friend of ours who manages a lot of employees had to fire someone. The manager made the mistake of not requiring her to turn over her computer files or keys to the office. The ex-employee returned over the weekend and destroyed every computer file in which she had been working.

Not everyone is going to do something like this. But in the heat of the moment, someone might try to destroy files that took months to put together. Or they might steal files, or grab client records, rolodex cards, and other items that might help them either build up their own business or tear yours down.

Take keys, insist on all files being handed over to you, do things that may seem unnecessarily cautious in order to protect your company's valuable records.

You won't lose anything because you are not popular right now anyway.

This is all part of the fun of being the boss.

Secret #206 Thank you. Gracias. Merci. Danke.

Pick whichever one flows off your tongue and use it liberally to let people know that you know how much work they did, and how much you appreciate their efforts.

Thanks.

Good job.

Great work there.

Way to go.

Proud of you.

Practice saying these phrases. It's surprising how much easier it is to say them, once you start.

Although some of our clients call when they get a finished piece from us, we don't hear a thing from many of them, unless they're calling to scream because it is not there on time. We assume, if we hear nothing, that everything is okay.

The ones who do call and tell us thanks are the ones for whom we can hardly wait to start another job. Everyone wants to feel appreciated. Nothing is more rewarding to someone who has done a project for you, or seen to it that something got done before the deadline, or went the extra mile to make sure it was right, than that you notice the effort and thank them for it.

Secret #207 What's that little sawing noise in back there?

You're going to have to go out on a limb sometimes in order to keep this whole show going. You will find it necessary to take chances, perhaps run a risk now and then. And when you take risks, you can lose. The flip side of that is that you can also win now and then.

For instance, you'll probably have to stand up to a client at some point. When we landed a new account that we had been working on for several months, one of the first things the new client wanted to meet with us about was our rate schedule.

She said that she thought our rates were too high and that everyone would be happy if we cut them in half.

We needed this account badly, but our response was instantaneous; we felt that our rates were the lowest in town for the type of specialized work that we did, and we could not lower them any more and still make a profit.

We had drawn a line in the corporate sandbox. We had to stand our ground.

What she was doing was trying to make herself look good to her boss at our expense.

What we were doing was trying to make her understand that no one could give her as good a deal as we could and still maintain the high quality work that we knew her company wanted to produce.

We talked about it for a while, then she backed off.

She could, I'm sure, have told us and her boss that it wasn't going to work out, and we probably would have lost the account before we even got to start on it. But I think that she realized that our rates were the lowest, and she maybe shouldn't rush us out the door so quickly.

Eventually we agreed that there were certain things she and her staff could do that would keep our total number of billing hours down, so that the amount we charged them would not exceed her budget. We knew that once she saw how good our work was and realized how much she could trust us, we could even raise our rates and it would be okay.

It's an old thought, but I think it's still a good one—people respect you if you respect yourself.

Secret #208   You gotta give a little.

If you want to get the best out of people who work with you, share your success with unexpected goodies every now and then.

I don't mean that you should send a private limo to pick up employees each morning. But there are other, more reasonable things you could do.

A forward-thinking president of an association in D.C. has started a summer hours tradition each year that all the employees look forward to and thoroughly enjoy. Starting the week of Memorial Day, everyone comes in a half-hour earlier Monday through Friday, and works through the lunch hour on Friday. Then the office shuts down at 1:00 P.M. on Friday afternoons.

It's wonderful—people can get a jump start on their weekends and be out of town before rush hour, or catch up on errands and shopping, or take in an afternoon matinee, or play 18 holes of golf, anything at all.

Best of all, the attitude of the employees is much improved during the summer hours work week. Some put in more time and work harder than they do the rest of the year, just because they feel like it.

What can you do for your employees or freelancers that would motivate them to do better work? Here are a few ideas that you may want to consider:

- A free shopping day, a few weeks before Christmas or Hanukkah, with pay

- Paid vacation time for the part-timers

- A monthly lunch on the company

- A bonus check with the paycheck when you know that extra effort has been put into something. It doesn't have to be a fortune—just $50 or $100 means a lot to people.

- Fresh-cut flowers or bright balloons for no reason

- Pay tuition and even give time off for work-related courses at local colleges and universities if an employee wants to do this.

Secret #209 Put your mouth where your money is.

What's that? You say you don't think it matters to the client whether or not you guarantee satisfaction with your work?

Think again.

You might as well hang up huge neon arrows that blink and point at you and read CONTRACT THIS PERSON AT YOUR OWN RISK.

A policy statement by you that if the client is not satisfied with your best efforts, they will not have to pay (or they won't have to pay nearly as much) is your insurance policy in good times and bad. I believe that most clients need to be reassured that they're going to look good, and this helps.

It's all interconnected, like some life-size jigsaw puzzle. Some person is waiting for this part, or those figures, or that printed piece from you, and someone else is waiting for a piece from them, so they can do their job or put out their publication or set up their trade show booth.

I occasionally need to call photographers who are complete strangers and ask them to shoot photos for us in places such as Paperclip, Arkansas, and Toejam, Wyoming. I used to worry about whether or not they'd come through, worry that the shots would be terrible, worry that someone would abuse our Federal Express number. But nobody has ever let us down, and as far as I know, no one ever stole our FedEx number, which is 9999999999999. Most of them have told us they guarantee our satisfaction or we don't have to pay.

Maybe it's American photographers as a breed—they're the greatest.

By telling your client you want them, above all, to be happy with your efforts, you enhance your image, and you come across as being self-assured about the quality of the work you do, which transfers to everyone involved, and you have a client who's going to have no reason to look anywhere else.

Secret #210 The jerk factor.

As sure as termites crawl up in the spring, there are going to be jerks who try to abuse your good business policy of guaranteeing your work.

You'll know it when it happens.

There will be a phone call weeks after your bill has gone out, or you'll have to call about the check because it's so late. And then you'll hear that the president/CEO/head honcho did not approve the bill because she/he felt it was way too high for the work involved, or because somebody's secretary said that it could have been done in Toledo for a tenth of what you charged, or some other nincompoop reason.

It won't matter that you spent far more time on this job than you billed them for; it won't matter that you did the detail work for it, or that you double-proofed it and caught a lot of mistakes that the client let slip through; it won't matter that you saved them a fortune because of the way you did it or the method you used to get it done.

They want you to agree to accept half the amount, or one-third of the amount, or whatever.

Not everyone is going to agree with this, but my advice the first time this happens is to be a good sport and roll with it, take whatever they will give you. Cut your losses, hope your out-of-pocket expenses are covered, and try to add some more money into the next job you get from this account.

That is, if you want a next job from this account.

If you feel like cutting their rolodex card into confetti and could easily make it through life without ever seeing them again, raise your rates on any other estimate they might ask you for so they won't give you more work.

There are too many good ones out there for you to get stuck with this kind of loser.

Secret #211 How's your sex life, and other totally irrelevant questions.

When you think about it, none of your business is anyone else's business.

But people are going to ask you questions you won't believe they would have the nerve to ask. Here are some of the things we've been asked, and the responses I wish I'd thought of at the time:

Q. *How much money do you guys earn every year?*

A. Enough.

Q. *Come on, really? As much as you could earn at a regular job?*

A. What's a regular job? One where you commute for three hours every day and work for someone you loathe? Where the office politics make Capitol Hill look like the comatose ward? Where you have to spend half your salary on clothes and the other half on day care and cleaning? Get real.

Q. *Well, what about benefits? Do you guys have any, working for yourselves and all?*

A. That's certainly a big one, don't you think?

Q. *(He's a guy, so he glances down) Yes, it is, isn't it?*

A. Don't make me laugh, I've just had major gut surgery and I might explode all over you. We were talking about benefits.

Q. *(Looking at your portfolio) What did this piece cost to produce?*

A. Enough.

Q. *What kind of money do these people spend every year?*

A. We don't talk about any of our clients, ever.

Q. *How much money did you guys have when you started your business?*

A. Why don't you buy and read my first book, *Be the Boss*. It'll tell you everything about that.

Secret #212 G*W*T*F*

Time after time, we've seen breathlessly happy, pink-cheeked entrepreneurs rushing out in the heady, early days, optimistically waving around contracts from new accounts, securing huge lines of credit from the bank, borrowing from everywhere to buy expensive pieces of equipment, signing long-term leases in places with names like Ye Olde Towne Square Malle that offer undergrounde parkinge and a healthe clube on the premises.

And in a year or so, they're letting people go, trying to get out of the lease, selling the expensive equipment for a small fraction of what it's worth, looking grimmer and grayer, then dropping out of sight as collection agencies start coming around.

This is what can happen when you bite off more than you can handle. The big secret here is that you are going to worry less, have more energy to devote to your business, and have a better chance at survival if you:

- are careful, watch every penny that goes out;
- don't greedily take advantage of every credit pitch that you ever get in the mail;
- spend small, keep your overhead costs and salaries very low; and
- learn to go* with* the* flow.*

I know a lot of guys, particularly those of the male persuasion, are going to disagree with this; most of them are working for a large company and think that once they break away and start their own company, they are going to be the exception to this rule. Since you can't tell any-body anything, I won't comment.

Finances and Taxes

Secret #213 Ten easy ways to raise your rates while keeping your customer happy.

And if you scratch the bottom of this page, it will turn into a million dollar bill.

Ever since the age of decadence (A.D. 37 to 41, Caligula's reign as emperor, not the 1980s), your clients have had to justify every dollar spent on outside costs, while trying to explain to their employees why they can't have more than a half percent raise this year—which they should feel lucky to get, seeing as how a lot of people are without jobs.

There is no painless way to raise your rates.

There are, however, a few ways to get paid more fairly for the work you are doing. Just don't call it a rate increase.

If you're not billing enough of your time, try to gradually increase your hours. Don't jump up 100 hours in one month, but add on another couple of hours this month, then a few more next month.

Which services do you give away? Most of us do some work for which we don't charge. Do you back-up proof your client's work, or make a ton of phone calls, or deliver packages or envelopes in person, or attend meetings with them?

Add a new category to your bill for this service, and charge a fair amount. Most clients, whether they tell you this or not, appreciate that you're doing extra work for them and won't mind approving a new charge for some of that extra work, as long as it's reasonable.

Well, okay, some clients are that way.

Alright—one. There's gotta be one.

If you really have to raise your hourly rates, be sure to let the client know well in advance—at least 90 days ahead of time—that you have to do it. Most clients must stick to a budget each fiscal year, and this gives them time to make adjustments in what they have left to spend.

Or they'll just completely ignore your warning and not deal with it, then ask you to cut your prices later when they realize their budget went through the roof.

Speaking of which, try to find out when budget-planning time is for your client. It shouldn't be too hard. It's that time of year when their personality changes into one with all the charm of a starving lion, and you'll get brief calls late at night where they say something like, "Quick—get all the figures together for the blah-blah convention within the next 30 seconds and call me back."

The absolute worst thing you can do is try and sneak a higher rate onto the bill and hope they won't notice. They'll see it. Clients might not notice if you walk into the meeting in a clown suit and with your hair on fire, but they'll notice a tiny rate increase, believe me.

On the other hand, this is an excellent way to get rid of a client you don't want to keep.

Secret #214 You may have more connections than you want.

You know the feeling that comes over you when you realize the person to whom you've been sending the copy of the overdue $5,000 invoice for six months may not intend to pay you.

Almost as if you've been betrayed.

No, make that exactly. You *have* been betrayed.

You have a genuine deadbeat on your hands.

There are a number of things you can aggressively do to try to get your money—make a complete pest of yourself by phone, drag some of your largest, meanest-looking friends with you to the client's office, and take the deadbeat to small claims court. But be careful not to blab about him to swarthy-looking guys whose last names end in a vowel, and who offer to hook you up with the right people who could scare the spit out of whoever may need the spit scared out of them.

It's not that I didn't believe the mob existed. I mean, come on—I've seen all *The Godfather* movies, as well as *Crimes and Misdemeanors* and *Married to the you-know-who*. I did, however, believe that this *very fine* group of business people could only be seen at such places as shipping docks and Italian restaurants that specialize in red sauces, until this particular day when I was talking with a man—never mind who or where—and dumping my collection woes on him. He was very sweet, really, and I'm sure he only meant to help me.

Now that I think about it, it was a fine human gesture.

Much appreciated.

But what he did was, he scared the spit out of me. Because I knew he meant it. He could have some people get in touch with the deadbeat and convince him to pay up or lose his teeth. It's weird to talk one-on-one with someone who would really do this. Frightened suddenly, I said no thanks and cleared out of there pretty fast. And I've kept my mouth shut about our collection problems. It's no one else's business anyway.

P.S. The deadbeat did pay up—finally. Does that make him a livebeat? And he still has all of his teeth, as far as I know.

Secret #215 I'll have another frangi-pangi, please.

When you're paying the client for the privilege of working for them, something is wrong. This is not the way things should work in the business world, except if you're a maitre d' earning low-to-middle six figures at certain restaurants in Manhattan.

This is the way this type of thing can happen:

1. The client asks you to do a project.

2. You leap in, do everything the client has asked for, including hiring a professional to help you, and you pay that person for his/her time.

3. Client looks at your presentation, says it's great, decides to make minor adjustments here and there.

4. Repeat step 2.

5. Repeat step 3.

6. You repeat step 2, only you are spending more for out-of-pocket things such as couriers, proofs, supplies, etc.

7. Repeat step 3, except this time the minor adjustments become major changes in the structure of the job.

8. You have arrived at the point where you are now paying the client to do his or her work. (Actually, you arrived at this point the first time you reached step 2, only you didn't know it.)

If things have gotten this bad, you have two choices—either bill the client for all your work so far, including every out-of-pocket cost you have incurred; or keep letting the expenses pile up until you are too embarrassed to bill the client for so much money, so you settle for a much lower amount, when and if this job ever reaches completion.

In an ideal world, you would have given the client an estimate between step 2 and step 3 and made sure the client understood that costs were only going up from there. However, it's not always easy to do this. I know. You're looking at somebody who could have retired young and been living in Bora Bora if I had billed all our clients for all the actual work we ever did for them.

Secret #216 Let me say this about estimating a project, then I promise that's it, okay?

Remember these points when you estimate the cost of a project.

1. If it's anything you care about, you'll put more time into it than you ever imagined, so try to build a little extra money into the estimated cost.

2. The primary hold-up to beginning any job is usually that the client has not signed the estimate yet. (Good for you. Keep holding it up until they do.)

3. Nothing is easy; you only make it look easy because you are ultra professional, and above all, a wonderful person.

4. Somewhere along the way, some clients will make changes. Because they forget everything when it's over except how to take complete credit, *you must tell them as you go* that they'll have to pay more. For added relief, stick out your tongue as she/he leaves the room.

5. Outside costs go up between the time that you get the client to approve the estimate and when you receive your vendors' bills.

6. Running a small business is tough, but so are you.

7. The client may decide, halfway through, that this job is totally unnecessary or that someone else (in-

house) could do it for a quarter of the price. Offer to trim wherever possible, depending on which stage the job is in, but don't just walk away from it without charging for all outside expenses, plus some amount for your time. You will have absolutely no respect from your client or for yourself if you don't fight for what you have earned.

8. Although you may never be as rich as you dream of being, remind yourself why you went into business on your own—to remain independent, so that you don't ever have to work for some cheap sleazebag like your client who is slashing everything down to the core.

9. You will probably not be thanked, but you can make an effort to tell all the people who worked with you that they did a good job, which will make you feel better.

10. Most clients won't ever pay as soon as you hope they will.

11. Weeks later, you'll call about the check to find out the holdup was that the client had a question about one part of a $17,000 bill, such as a $15 courier fee.

12. You'll be asked to bid on another project for the same client before you have a chance to breathe.

Secret #217   Comma ci, comma ca.

As the owner of a small business, you have exactly the same headaches as the president of GM or CBS or Dogs 'n Suds—payroll, health insurance and other benefits, billings, invoicing, client problems, employee problems, management hassles, white collar theft, blue collar theft, pink collar theft, in fact, theft of all colors of collars, profit/loss statements that show more loss than profit, not enough supplies on hand, strikes that threaten your business, too much work, not enough work, collars that have too much starch, and of course, people who wear no collars.

The only difference in your business and many of America's top companies is the number of commas in your company's annual profits.

You'll probably have more.

Secret #218 The Cisco Kid was a friend of mine until we formed a partnership and then we had a big fight.

Be sure to have a buy-and-sell agreement written into your contract when you form a partnership, or you may experience Horrible Surprise #98.

If you have set up a partnership with the Cisco Kid, and you don't have a buy-and-sell agreement (also called a buy-sell clause), your business goes bye-bye if old Cisco kicks the bucket. Cisco doesn't even have to kick the bucket; if he just gets mad and walks away, your business is suddenly an ex-business.

This does not apply to companies that are incorporated. This is unique to partnerships, whether comprised of two people or 20 people.

It has long been known that people named the Cisco Kid die, or at least get mad. A buy-and-sell agreement spells out what will happen after this occurrence, which partner(s) will buy Cisco's share, and how much that share would be worth.

You can take out an insurance policy to cover the cost of buying out Cisco, but here's Horrible Surprise #99—the cost of the policy is not tax-deductible. In fact, it seems that partnerships are not a great idea in general, tax-wise speaking. Although the business pays no federal tax, each partner files as if she/he is a proprietor and pays normal tax rates, plus self-employment tax.

Just as each partner can rake in a share of all the profits

from the company, so each partner is equally responsible for all debts and any taxes that local and state jurisdictions decide to collect.

So why do people form partnerships with guys named the Cisco Kid? Money is the bottom line here. It's easier for five people to raise $10,000 each than it is for one person to raise $50,000.

Secret #219 A tiny break for self-employed people.

It's not much, but it helps. As of 1990, the IRS changed the self-employment tax to 15.3%, and as of 1991, we paid this up to a maximum of $53,400 on our net earnings.

The good news here is that you can deduct half of this self-employment tax amount, or 7.65%, as a business expense when you figure your adjusted gross income, as well as when you fill out your lovely Schedule SE. This is an income tax deduction only, not a deduction when you figure net earnings. But it helps.

Secret #220 And now about that business interruptus policy.

Paying for insurance is a real drag. Just when you think the company has an extra $2,000 or $3,000 to stash away in a CD, along comes the old liability, disability, fire and casualty, worker's comp, crime, theft, life or employee health insurance bill. Or all of them at once.

The thing that kills me about insurance is that the entire concept goes against normal human nature, much like roller coasters, girdles, and lime-flavored gelatin. Our natural inclination is to have no insurance, to be naked as jaybirds, to take our chances. We want to believe that nothing will happen to us, that we're lucky, that the stars are in our favor.

But the insurance salespeople drag out these charts and figures, hand us thickly bound reports that show what tremendous risks we are taking just by getting out of bed in the morning, and interject the phrase "God forbid" in between every third word. It's possible that they force this negative energy into our lives by just reminding us of the fragility of it all.

Here are some ways you can try to cut back on the costs of premiums:

1. Take out the biggest deductibles you can possibly get. It's probably going to be cheaper to replace a small computer or piece of equipment that gets stolen or broken than to claim it and get a whopper of a premium increase next year. How much can you afford to spend to replace everything? If you can spend several thousand dollars, then make that your deductible.

Same is true with health insurance—your premiums are much more affordable if you can carry a $500 to $1,000 deductible.

2. Take advantage of the free credit card insurance programs. Several of the major credit companies offer to replace anything you buy using their credit card, no matter what happens to it, and some extend this coverage up to two years. Remember, though, that this usually is not automatic. You have to request the forms to be mailed to you, then fill them out and mail them back with the receipts, then wait to receive them back, stamped and official.

3. Work at home. A business owner's policy can cost less when you run a company from your home, because you can broaden the liability coverage on your homeowner's or apartment dweller's policy. Check the language of the policy and endorsements to make sure your business interests are covered, and remember to salt those steps and shovel that sidewalk.

Secret #221 Isn't that a
convenience store?

Who is filing all those Chapter 7 and Chapter 11 bankruptcies?

So many businesses that there's a whole new profitable line of work for bankruptcy attorneys, as well as one hot market for commercial lenders, but this is not the real question here.

The real question here is, what is the difference between a Chapter 7 and a Chapter 11 bankruptcy? No, the answer is not four chapters.

Chapter 7 is total and complete financial ruin. Utter liquidity. The owner/s admit/s there is no possible way ever to become profitable again, and a court trustee sells any assets that the company owns (normally worth about $45) to pay off claims to creditors (usually adding up to somewhere in the millions). You will notice there is something of a difference there, dollar-wise speaking. This negative base of capital is what we laughingly call "the economy."

Chapter 11 is kind of like swimming with a big innertube, but all around you are these shark-like things.

Oh—plus you have cut your leg and it's bleeding.

The company that files Chapter 11 has to be able to prove in court that there is hope, that it can figure out a way to distract the sharks long enough to make it back to shore which, if you've ever seen a James Bond movie, you know can be done quite easily.

For companies that have been badly managed or have hit a streak of bad luck, sometimes the only dignified way out is to declare bankruptcy. (Why do people *declare* bankruptcy? Does this show that they really really really mean it?) If the company is incorporated, only the assets of the company are involved. If the company is a sole proprietorship or partnership, then the assets of the owners can be seized (gasp!) and used to pay back creditors.

So children, the moral of this story is to eat your green leafy vegetables and don't spend money you don't have.

Secret #222 The FUTA-ility of it all.

Ah, good old Employer's Annual Federal Unemployment Tax Return, or FUTA Form 940, now with the addition of tiny but mighty Form 940-EZ to its stable.

FUTA is the money that the federal government collects from businesses in each state to make up for the unemployment that the feds give to the states. For the first $7,000 you pay yourself, your partner, and each of your employees, you must pay .008 to FUTA, not .062, or 6.2%, which is what I wrote in the first *Be the Boss*.

Even with the easier Form 940-EZ, FUTA is a pain in the astronomical game of life. Sometime in 1990, the IRS sent me one of their scary-looking letters with the words URGENT—PAYMENT REQUIRED at the top, claiming that I had not paid FUTA for 1989. I checked my records, and of course, I had paid it. I wrote them back and enclosed a copy of the check (front and back). They then wrote me that they still had not received my FUTA payment for 1989, and they were adding interest.

It was time to get personal.

I called the local IRS office and got someone who transferred me to the Baltimore regional office, where I asked if I could speak with someone—anyone—who might be knowledgeable about FUTA.

"What?" she asked.

"FUTA—that's F-U-T-A. I need to talk to someone who knows about it."

"Just a moment, please." She put me on hold.

IRS muzak played.

The mail was delivered.

The cat climbed the windows by way of the horizontal blinds.

Finally, another woman picked up the line.

"Hello?" she asked.

"Yes?" I replied eagerly, thinking that at last I was getting somewhere with this mess, that here was the person who could straighten all this out and make it go away.

"Is this Miss FUTA?" she asked.

At least she pronounced it correctly, even if it was not my name.

And here's something really cool about another type of employment tax—the amount we pay in unemployment to the District of Columbia had been decreasing gradually for the past few years, and finally bottomed out at a very low rate. Want to know why?

Because the way unemployment works, the fewer times that people are hired and fired in your company, the less money you have to pay for unemployment insurance. This is supposed to be true nationwide.

Now if only health, home, and auto insurance companies would follow this lead.

Secret #223 The big secret that the IRS doesn't want you to know.

Ever since I called the IRS at 3:30 on a weekday afternoon several years ago and got the cleaning woman, I've known what that big secret is, the one that the government manages to keep from us: they're all human, just like us.

I have regularly sent in our quarterly 941 forms, our yearly 940 (FUTA) forms, filed W-2s and W-3s, and paid taxes on time each year, and they have done things like apply a payment to another account, then said I didn't pay it, then billed me for the amount plus interest.

They will make mistakes, just as they always have, and it is your duty as an American citizen to straighten them out. What you have to do is read the form they send you, *no matter how scary it looks,* and then respond within 30 days.

It will probably have a message at the top that says FINAL WARNING or SECOND NOTICE. Of course, you never got the early warning or the first notice because who knows why.

Along with the information about how you didn't pay them on time (which you did, and you have the cancelled checks to prove it) will probably be some kind of message about how the fine for ignoring this particular notice could be something like a million dollars and/or the rest of your life in prison.

Puh-lease.

When I got my FINAL NOTICE (this was the first time I'd seen it) from the IRS about the payment that they said I owed them (which had been paid), I typed a letter and enclosed copies of my check (front and back) and a copy of their notice. I said in the letter that they should stop using scary tactics such as this, that it wasn't very nice, and it could cause some people to really freak.

Several weeks later, I received what you could possibly call an apology, where they wrote that they did see that my payment had been misapplied by someone in their office, and they had corrected their records and were dropping all interest charges.

They didn't say a thing about changing their scary tactics.

But just so you know—they maik mistrakes jus like you 'n me.

Secret #224 YBTK–your neat little package from the IRS.

Your Business Tax Kit (YBTK) is your complimentary gift from the federal government for starting up your own business. Okay, okay, it's not a tennis bracelet or a red Mercedes convertible, but hey—you don't have to look at the federal government over your coffee every morning, either. That would be one butt-ugly sight, plus it probably wouldn't even carry its own cup back to the sink.

What is included in YBTK and shown here is the following:

1. Publication 334, *Tax Guide for Small Business*

2. Publication 509, *Tax Calendars*

3. Publication 583, *Taxpayers Starting a Business*

4. Publication 910, *Guide to Free Tax Services*

5. A check for a million dollars

6. Just seeing if you're paying attention. This is the Sargasso Sea part of the book

7. Publication 937, *Business Reporting*

8. Publication 1057, *Small Business Tax Education Program brochure*

9. Publication 454-A, *YBTK Content Sheet*

10. Form SS-4, Application for Employer Identification Number

11. Form 1040-ES, Estimated Tax for Individuals

12. And a partridge in a pear tree.

Also shown in this section are a few other forms that the IRS believes can be of use to you. You can call the IRS at **1-800-TAX-FORMS (1-800/829-3676)** to request any of these publications.

If you're considering an office in your home, be sure to call and ask for Publication 587, *Business Use of Your Home*. This fascinating booklet describes exactly what you can and can't deduct when you run a business from your home, and it explains Form 8829, *Expenses for Business Use of Your Home*, which must be filed with Schedule C. It's a lovely form, really, it is.

The IRS is extremely helpful when it comes to sending you the right forms. You call the toll-free number, the forms are in your mailbox in a few weeks. This part is fabulous. The only teeny-tiny problem you may encounter is when you try to read and understand the forms, and then fill them all out.

In fact, I just this second realized that my best advice to you in regard to all these tax forms is to find a good accountant and let her or him figure it all out for you. I don't mean the quarterly and yearly forms that I described in detail in the first *Be the Boss*—those aren't too bad. I mean the blasted tax forms.

Pay your accountant whatever he or she charges you—it's worth it if your tax forms are done properly. I figure, they went to college for a billion years just to learn what all the initials mean. Do you honestly think you can take a Saturday afternoon workshop down at your local college or IRS office and master this madness? Spend your time doing what you do best—no, not making Dagwood sandwiches—building up your business.

Tax Guide for Small Business

Income, Excise, and Employment Taxes for
Individuals, Partnerships, and Corporations

Department
of the
Treasury

Internal
Revenue
Service

Publication 334
Cat. No. 11063P

For use in
preparing
1991
Returns

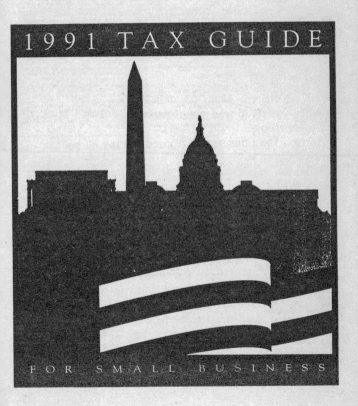

1991 TAX GUIDE

FOR SMALL BUSINESS

Department of the Treasury
Internal Revenue Service
Catalog Number 15013X

Publication 509
(Rev. Oct. 91)

Tax Calendars for 1992

Contents

Important Reminders

Deposit of excise taxes. For quarters beginning after March 31, 1991, Form 720 taxes that are subject to deposit requirements must be deposited semimonthly, regardless of the amount of tax liability. Monthly deposits of Form 720 taxes are no longer allowed. See *Form 720 Taxes* under *Excise Tax Calendar.*

Schedule A (Form 720). If you have an entry in Part 1 of Form 720, *Quarterly Federal Excise Tax Return*, you generally must file the Schedule A (Form 720) *Excise Tax Liability* with the return. See *Form 720 Taxes* under *Excise Tax Calendar.*

Introduction

The publication is divided into three main parts—a general tax calendar and two specialized tax calendars. First, use the general calendar; then, turn to the more specialized calendars if they apply to you. The three calendars are:

1) *General Tax Calendar*, beginning on this page. Use this calendar first.

2) *Employer's Tax Calendar*, beginning on page 3. Use this calendar if your business has any employees or if you must withhold income tax on gambling winnings.

3) *Excise Tax Calendar*, beginning on page 7. Use this calendar if your business must pay any excise taxes.

These three calendars explain when to file tax returns, pay estimated tax, apply for extensions, send in information returns, and do the other things that are required by federal tax laws. They cover the tax laws that apply to individuals, corporations, partnerships, and sole proprietorships. But they do not cover estate and gift taxes. Nor do they cover the reporting requirements for trusts, exempt organizations, or special types of corporations.

Free publications and forms. If you need information on a subject not covered in this publication, you may check our other free publications. To order publications and forms, call our toll-free telephone number 1-800-TAX-FORM (1-800-829-3676) or write the Internal Revenue Service (IRS) Forms Distribution Center for your area as shown in the income tax package.

General Information

The following brief explanations of tax deposits and due dates may be helpful to you in using the tax calendars.

Tax deposits. Most taxes must be paid when the return is due. But in some cases, you may have to deposit the tax before filing the return. Tax deposits are figured for periods of time that are shorter than the time period covered by the return. See *Deposits* under *Employer's Tax Calendar* and under *Excise Tax Calendar,* later.

Deposits must be made at an authorized financial institution or a Federal Reserve bank. A deposit received after the due date will be considered timely if you can establish that it was mailed at least two days before the due date. However, deposits of $20,000 or more by an employer required to deposit the tax more than once a month must be received by the due date to be timely.

Declaration of Independence

Each deposit must be accompanied by a federal tax deposit coupon. You can get the coupons you need by calling or writing the IRS.

Tax deposit coupons. For all tax deposits, you must use Form 8109, *Federal Tax Deposit Coupon.* Each coupon has fill-in spaces for indicating the type of tax you are depositing and the tax quarter for which the deposit is being made. Use a separate coupon for each type of tax you are depositing. For example, if you must deposit taxes for both excise taxes reported on Form 720 and federal unemployment taxes reported on Form 940, you must use a separate coupon for each tax and mark each coupon to indicate the tax you are depositing.

Saturday, Sunday, or legal holiday. Generally, if a due date that is set by law falls on a Saturday, Sunday, or legal holiday, it is delayed until the next day that is not a Saturday, Sunday, or legal holiday. These calendars make the adjustment for Saturdays, Sundays, and federal holidays. But you must make any adjustments for statewide holidays. (Exceptions to this rule for excise taxes are noted later.)

Statewide holidays. A statewide legal holiday delays a due date only if the IRS office where you are required to file is located in that state.

Penalties. Whenever possible, you should take action *before* the listed due date. If you are late, you may have to pay a penalty as well as interest on any overdue taxes.

In addition to civil penalties, criminal penalties may be imposed for intentionally not paying taxes, for intentionally filing a false return, or for not filing a required return.

General Tax Calendar

This tax calendar has the due dates for 1992 that most taxpayers will need. Business employers and businesses that pay excise taxes should also use the *Employer's Tax Calendar* (page 3) and the *Excise Tax Calendar* (page 7).

Fiscal-year taxpayers. If you file your income tax return for a fiscal year rather than the calendar year, you must change some of the dates in this calendar. These changes are described under *Fiscal-Year Taxpayers* at the end of this calendar.

Employers of household workers. If you have hired someone to work in your home rather than in your business—for example, to do child care, housekeeping, or gardening work—you may have to pay the employer's share of social security and Medicare taxes (FICA taxes) tax and also withhold the employee's share from his or her wages. If your employee agrees, you can also withhold income tax. These taxes are due quarterly on Form 942, *Employer's Quarterly Tax Return for Household Employees.* This calendar includes the due dates for filing Form 942.

You may also have to pay federal unemployment (FUTA) tax for your household employees. In addition, they may be eligible to receive advance payments of the earned income credit from you. See Publication 926, *Employment Taxes for Household Employees,* for more information.

First Quarter

The first quarter of a calendar year is made up of January, February, and March.

January 10

Employees who work for tips. If you received $20 or more in tips during December, report them to your employer. You can use Form 4070.

Department of the Treasury
Internal Revenue Service
Catalog Number 15150B

Publication 583

Taxpayers Starting a Business

For use in preparing
1991 Returns

Contents

Important Change for 1991

Business use of your home. Beginning in 1991, if you use part of your home for your trade or business and can deduct the expenses on Schedule C (Form 1040), you must figure your deduction on Form 8829, *Expenses for Business Use of Your Home*, and attach it to Schedule C. For more information, see Publication 587, *Business Use of Your Home*.

Introduction

This publication discusses several topics of interest to an individual starting a small business. It covers the following topics:

- Types of Businesses
- Identification Numbers
- Business Taxes
- Information Returns
- Records

The publication looks at some of the decisions you must make when setting up a recordkeeping system, and the types of books and records included in a typical system for a small business. Sample records and filled-in forms are illustrated at the end of the publication.

Penalties. To ensure that all taxpayers pay their fair share of taxes, the law provides penalties for failure to file returns or pay taxes as required. Other penalties that may be charged include those pointed out later under *Business Taxes* and *Information Returns*. You may not be charged a penalty if your noncompliance was due to reasonable cause.

However, criminal penalties may be imposed for willful failure to file, tax evasion, or making a false statement.

Free publications and forms. If you need information on a subject not covered in this publication, you can check our other free publications. For a subject matter index to IRS publications and information about other free tax services, see Publication 910, *Guide to Free Tax Services*.

To order publications and forms, call our toll-free telephone number 1-800-TAX-FORM

(1-800-829-3676) or write the IRS Forms Distribution Center for your area as shown in the income tax package.

Types of Businesses

When you begin a business, you must decide which type of business entity to use. Legal and tax considerations will enter into this decision. However, legal considerations are beyond the scope of this publication.

Normally, a business is conducted in the form of a sole proprietorship, partnership, or corporation. If your business is a sole proprietorship or partnership, the business itself does not pay income tax. The sole proprietor or the partners include the profit or loss on their personal tax returns. The profit of a corporation, except for an S corporation, is taxed both to the corporation and to the shareholders when the profit is distributed as dividends. But, any loss of the corporation, except for an S corporation, is generally not deductible by its stockholders.

Sole proprietorships. A sole proprietorship is the simplest form of business organization. The business has no existence apart from you, the owner. Its liabilities are your personal liabilities and you undertake the risks of the business for all assets owned, whether used in the business or personally owned.

You must report the profit or loss from each of your businesses operated as a sole proprietorship on a separate Schedule C (Form 1040), *Profit or Loss From Business*, and the combined profit or loss is entered on Form 1040.

As a sole proprietor, you may be liable for self-employment tax and may have to make estimated tax payments.

For more information on sole proprietorships, see Publication 334, *Tax Guide for Small Business*.

Partnerships. A partnership is not a taxable entity. However, a partnership must figure its profit or loss and file a return on Form 1065, *U.S. Partnership Return of Income*.

A partnership is the relationship existing between two or more persons who join together to carry on a trade or business. Each person contributes money, property, labor, or skill, and expects to share in the profits and losses of the business.

For more information, see Publication 541, *Tax Information on Partnerships*.

Corporations. Forming a corporation involves a transfer of either money, property, or both, by the prospective shareholders in exchange for capital stock in the corporation. Most corporations file Form 1120, *U.S. Corporation Income Tax Return*, or Form 1120-A, *U.S. Corporation Short-Form Income Tax Return*. A corporation generally takes the same deductions as a sole proprietorship to figure its taxable income. A corporation is also entitled to special deductions.

For more information, see Publication 542, *Tax Information on Corporations*.

S corporations. A qualifying corporation may choose to be generally exempt from federal income tax. Its shareholders will then include in their income their share of the corporation's separately stated items of income, deduction, loss, and credit, and their share of nonseparately stated income or loss. A corporation that makes this choice is known as an S corporation.

To make this election, a corporation must have no more than 35 shareholders, in addition to other requirements. An S corporation files its return on Form 1120S, *U.S. Income Tax Return for an S Corporation*.

For more information, see Publication 589, *Tax Information on S Corporations*.

Declaration of Independence.

When in the Course of human events one people to dissolve the political bands which connect them with another, and to assume among the powers of the earth, the separate and equal

Department
of the
Treasury
Internal
Revenue
Service

Guide to Free Tax Services

Inside: Free Publications, Free Phone Service,
Free Person-to-Person Assistance, and
Tax Return Filing Tips

Publication 910 (Rev. 11-91)
Catalog Number 15315 W

FOR TAX YEAR 1991

Department of the Treasury
Internal Revenue Service
Catalog Number 63126N

Publication 937

Business Reporting

- Employment Taxes
- Information Returns

For use in preparing
1991 Returns

Declaration of Independence

When in the Course of human events it becomes necessary for one people to dissolve the political bands which have connected them with another, and to assume among the powers of the earth, the separate and equal station to which the Laws of Nature and of

Contents

Important Changes for 1991

Social security and Medicare taxes. Beginning in 1991, the computation of social security tax is separated into two parts. The old-age, survivors, and disability insurance part is referred to as social security. The hospital insurance part is referred to as Medicare. You must report each of these items separately on Forms 941 and W-2.

The tax rate for social security is 6.2% each for employers and employees (12.4% total) and the wage base for 1991 is $53,400. For 1992, the wage base is $55,500.

The tax rate for Medicare is 1.45% each for employers and employees (2.9% total) and the wage base for 1991 is $125,000. For 1992, the wage base is $130,200.

Form 1099-R replaces Form W-2P. Form W-2P, *Statement for Recipients of Annuities, Pensions, Retired Pay, or IRA Payments,* is obsolete after 1990. The information that was on the 1990 Form W-2P has been added to the 1991 Form 1099-R, *Distributions From Pensions, Annuities, Retirement or Profit-Sharing Plans, IRAs, Insurance Contracts, etc.* File the 1991 Form 1099-R with the Internal Revenue Service (IRS) by February 28, 1992, with Form 1096, *Annual Summary and Transmittal of U.S. Information Returns.*

Group legal service plans. Under the *Tax Extension Act of 1991,* the cost of group legal service plans is not subject to social security, Medicare, federal unemployment taxes, and income tax withholding if the cost is paid before July 1, 1992, for periods before that date. See *Withholding and Reporting Payments Other Than Wages* under *Income Tax Withholding.*

Educational assistance plans. Under the *Tax Extension Act of 1991,* the cost of educational assistance plans is not subject to social security, Medicare, federal unemployment taxes, and income tax withholding if the cost is paid before July 1, 1992. See *Withholding and Reporting Payments Other Than Wages* under *Income Tax Withholding.*

Federal unemployment (FUTA) tax rate. The gross FUTA tax rate remains at 6.2% through 1992.

Introduction

This publication is mainly designed for small businesses. This includes self-employed persons such as sole-proprietors, independent contractors, and members of a partnership.

Free publications and forms. If you need information on a subject not covered in this publication, please check our other free publications. To order publications and forms, call our toll-free telephone number, 1-800-TAX-FORM (1-800-829-3676). You may also write to the IRS Forms Distribution Center for your area as shown in the income tax package.

Employment Taxes

If you have any employees, you will probably be required to withhold federal income tax from their wages. You may also have to withhold and pay social security and Medicare taxes. If you do not withhold these taxes, or withhold the taxes but do not deposit them, you may be subject to a penalty equal to the amount of the tax. See *Penalties* under *Deposits,* later.

This publication discusses an employer's responsibility for these taxes. It also discusses income tax withholding on payments other than wages, the federal unemployment (FUTA) tax, the rules for advance payment of the earned income credit, and the rules for tip reporting and allocation. Information useful for 1992 is also included.

If you need information on railroad taxes, see the instructions for Form CT-1, *Employer's Annual Railroad Retirement and Unemployment Repayment Tax Return,* and Form CT-2, *Employee Representative's Quarterly Railroad Tax Return.* Railroad retirement and railroad unemployment repayment taxes are explained in the Instructions for Form CT-1.

Note. After your employees file their 1991 income tax returns, you can help them correct any mistakes they may have made in figuring their income tax withholding for 1991 by making new 1992 Forms W-4 available. You should encourage them to check their income tax withholding situation if they owed a large amount of tax or received a large refund for 1991, and to give you a new Form W-4 for 1992 if necessary. An employee is most likely to have too little tax withheld if both the employee and his or her spouse work. See *Form W-4 Withholding Allowances,* under *Income Tax Withholding,* later.

After you receive completed Forms W-4 from your employees, you can help them determine whether they are having the right amount of income tax withheld in 1992 by giving them Publication 919, *Is My Withholding Correct for 1992?* This publication will help your employees compare the amount of tax they expect to show on their 1992 tax returns with the amount of tax to be withheld from their pay during 1992.

Employee's social security number. If one of your employees does not have a social security number and has not applied for one, you should tell the employee to submit an application on Form SS-5, *Application for a Social Security Card,* to the nearest Social Security office. Also, if an employee has changed his or her name, he or she should ask the Social Security Administration for a corrected social security card. Form SS-5 can be obtained from any Social Security office.

If any of your employees are under 18 years old, they must furnish evidence of age, identity, and U.S. citizenship along with the Form SS-5. Employees who are 18 years old or older must appear in person with this evidence at a Social Security office.

Take a
STEP
in the right
direction for your
small business!

*a cooperative
effort to
provide business tax
education. . .*

Department of the Treasury
Internal Revenue Service
Publication 1057 (Rev 7-91)
Catalog Number 46913E

Your Business Tax Kit

Department of the Treasury
Internal Revenue Service
Publication 454-A (Rev. 9-91)
Cat. No. 46525S

Here's Your Business Tax Kit (YBTK) to help make your taxes less taxing. You have the right to know all you can about your Federal tax benefits and responsibilities. The forms and publications apply solely to Federal taxes, therefore, you should consult with state or local taxing authorities for their requirements. In your kit you'll find Publication 334, Tax Guide for Small Business, an easy to read business tax reference which explains situations that apply to a small business.

To find out about educational programs for small businesses, complete the interest form on the enclosed Publication 1057, Small Business Tax Education Program (STEP) Brochure, and mail it to the nearest IRS office listed for your state. Through a unique partnership between IRS and many community and junior colleges, universities and business associations across the country, small business owners (sole-proprietors, partnerships and corporations) have an opportunity to learn what they need to know about taxes. Often educational programs are offered in conjunction with a variety of Federal and State agencies providing you with one-stop assistance. Contact your local Taxpayer Education Coordinator to find out about other IRS tax services available for small businesses, such as Community Outreach Tax Education. For more information, review the enclosed Publication 910, Guide to Free Tax Services.

WARNING!

IN ORDER TO AVOID ADDITIONAL TAXES AND SUBSTANTIAL PENALTIES THERE ARE IMPORTANT FACTS YOU SHOULD KNOW.

1. Formation of a corporation or a partnership does not release you from personal liability associated with employment taxes.

2. Classification of employees as "contract labor" and/or failure to properly withhold and report employment taxes could result in additional taxes and large penalties to the officers and owners of a business.

3. Employers are required to obtain valid social security numbers from all workers.

4. Corporate officers are employees, not contract labor, and are subject to withholding taxes.

YBTK ORDER BLANK

Form W-4	Form 1040 Sch SE	Form 1120	Inst 1120-S Sch D	Pub 15
Form 940	Form 1065	Form 1120 Sch D	Form 1120-W	Pub 393
Form 941	Inst 1065	Inst 1120/1120-A	Form 2553	Pub 505
Form 1040		Form 1120-A	Inst 2553	Pub 541
Inst 1040	Form 1065 Sch D	Form 1120-S	Form 4562	Pub 542
Form 1040 Sch C	Form 1065 Sch K-1	Inst 1120-S	Inst 4562	Pub 589
Form 1040 Sch E	Inst 1065 Sch K-1	Form 1120-S Sch D		

Internal Revenue Service   YBTK

Name _____

Number and Street _____

City _____   State _____   Zip Code _____

Form SS-4
(Rev. April 1991)
Department of the Treasury
Internal Revenue Service

Application for Employer Identification Number

(For use by employers and others. Please read the attached instructions before completing this form.)

EIN

OMB No. 1545-0003
Expires 4-30-94

<table>
<tr><td colspan="3">1 Name of applicant (True legal name) (See instructions.)</td></tr>
<tr><td colspan="2">2 Trade name of business, if different from name in line 1</td><td>3 Executor, trustee, "care of" name</td></tr>
<tr><td colspan="2">4a Mailing address (street address) (room, apt., or suite no.)</td><td>5a Address of business (See instructions.)</td></tr>
<tr><td colspan="2">4b City, state, and ZIP code</td><td>5b City, state, and ZIP code</td></tr>
<tr><td colspan="3">6 County and state where principal business is located</td></tr>
<tr><td colspan="3">7 Name of principal officer, grantor, or general partner (See instructions.) ▶</td></tr>
</table>

8a Type of entity (Check only one box.) (See instructions.)

- ☐ Individual SSN
- ☐ REMIC
- ☐ State/local government
- ☐ Other nonprofit organization (specify) ▶
- ☐ Other (specify) ▶

- ☐ Personal service corp.
- ☐ National guard

- ☐ Estate
- ☐ Plan administrator SSN
- ☐ Other corporation (specify)
- ☐ Federal government/military
- If nonprofit organization enter GEN (if applicable)

- ☐ Trust
- ☐ Partnership
- ☐ Farmers' cooperative
- ☐ Church or church controlled organization

8b If a corporation, give name of foreign country (if applicable) or state in the U.S. where incorporated ▶

Foreign country

State

9 Reason for applying (Check only one box.)
- ☐ Started new business
- ☐ Hired employees
- ☐ Created a pension plan (specify type) ▶
- ☐ Banking purpose (specify) ▶

- ☐ Changed type of organization (specify) ▶
- ☐ Purchased going business
- ☐ Created a trust (specify) ▶
- ☐ Other (specify) ▶

10 Date business started or acquired (Mo., day, year) (See instructions.)

11 Enter closing month of accounting year. (See instructions.)

12 First date wages or annuities were paid or will be paid (Mo., day, year). **Note:** *If applicant is a withholding agent, enter date income will first be paid to nonresident alien. (Mo., day, year)* . . . . ▶

<table>
<tr><td>13 Enter highest number of employees expected in the next 12 months. Note: If the applicant does not expect to have any employees during the period, enter "0." . . . . ▶</td><td>Nonagricultural</td><td>Agricultural</td><td>Household</td></tr>
</table>

14 Principal activity (See instructions.) ▶

15 Is the principal business activity manufacturing?
If "Yes," principal product and raw material used ▶   ☐ Yes   ☐ No

16 To whom are most of the products or services sold? Please check the appropriate box.   ☐ Business (wholesale)
☐ Public (retail)   ☐ Other (specify) ▶   ☐ N/A

17a Has the applicant ever applied for an identification number for this or any other business? . . . . ☐ Yes   ☐ No
Note: *If "Yes," please complete lines 17b and 17c.*

17b If you checked the "Yes" box in line 17a, give applicant's true name and trade name, if different than name shown on prior application.

True name ▶   Trade name ▶

17c Enter approximate date, city, and state where the application was filed and the previous employer identification number if known.
Approximate date when filed (Mo., day, year) | City and state where filed   Previous EIN

Under penalties of perjury, I declare that I have examined this application, and to the best of my knowledge and belief, it is true, correct, and complete   Telephone number (include area code)

Name and title (Please type or print clearly.) ▶

Signature ▶   Date ▶

Note: *Do not write below this line.   For official use only.*

<table>
<tr><td>Please leave blank ▶</td><td>Geo.</td><td>Ind.</td><td>Class</td><td>Size</td><td>Reason for applying</td></tr>
</table>

For Paperwork Reduction Act Notice, see attached instructions.   Cat. No. 16055N   Form **SS-4** (Rev. 4-91)

Form 1040-ES

Estimated Tax for Individuals

Department of the Treasury
Internal Revenue Service

This package is primarily for first-time filers of estimated tax.

OMB No. 1545-0087

1992

Paperwork Reduction Act Notice

We ask for the information on the payment-vouchers to carry out the Internal Revenue laws of the United States. You are required to give us the information. We need it to ensure that you are complying with these laws and to allow us to figure and collect the right amount of tax.

The time needed to complete the worksheets and prepare and file the payment-vouchers will vary depending on individual circumstances. The estimated average time is: Recordkeeping, 1 hr., 19 min.; Learning about the law, 20 min.; Preparing the worksheets and payment-vouchers, 49 min.; Copying, assembling, and sending the payment-voucher to the IRS, 10 min. If you have comments concerning the accuracy of these time estimates or suggestions for making this package easier, we would be happy to hear from you. You can write to both the Internal Revenue Service, Washington, DC 20224, Attention: IRS Reports Clearance Officer, T:FP; and the Office of Management and Budget, Paperwork Reduction Project (1545-0087), Washington, DC 20503. DO NOT send the payment-vouchers to either of these offices. Instead, see Where To File Your Payment-Voucher on page 5.

Purpose of This Package

Use this package to figure and pay your estimated tax. Estimated tax is the method used to pay tax on income that is not subject to withholding; for example: earnings from self-employment, interest, dividends, rents, alimony, etc.

This package is primarily for first-time filers who are or may be subject to paying estimated tax. This package can also be used if you did not receive or have lost your preprinted 1040-ES package. The estimated tax worksheet on page 3 will help you figure the correct amount to pay. The vouchers in this package are for crediting your estimated tax payments to your account correctly. Use the Record of Estimated Tax Payments on page 5 to keep track of the payments you have made and the number and amount of your remaining payments.

After we receive your first payment-voucher from this package, we will mail you a preprinted 1040-ES package with your name, address, and social security number on each payment-voucher. Use the preprinted vouchers when you receive them to make your remaining estimated tax payments for the year. This will speed processing, reduce processing costs, and reduce the chance of errors.

Do not use the vouchers in this package to notify the IRS of a change of address. If you have a new address, get Form 8822, Change of Address, by calling 1-800-829-3676. Send the completed form to the Internal Revenue Service Center where you filed your last tax return.

Who Must Make Estimated Tax Payments

In most cases, you must make estimated tax payments if you expect to owe, after subtracting your withholding and credits, at least $500 in tax for 1992, and you expect your withholding and credits to be less than the **smaller** of:

● 90% of the tax shown on your 1992 tax return, or

● 100% of the tax shown on your 1991 tax return (the return must cover all 12 months).

Caution: If 100% of your 1991 tax is the **smaller** of the two amounts, see Limit on Use of Prior Year's Tax on this page for special rules that may apply to you.

Generally, you do not have to pay estimated tax if you were a U.S. citizen or resident alien for all of 1991 and you had no tax liability for the full 12-month 1991 tax year.

The estimated tax rules apply to:

● U.S. citizens and residents,

● Residents of Puerto Rico, the Virgin Islands, Guam, the Commonwealth of the Northern Mariana Islands, and American Samoa, and

● Nonresident aliens (use Form 1040-ES(NR)).

If you also receive salaries and wages, you can avoid having to make estimated tax payments by asking your employer to take more tax out of your earnings. To do this, file a new **Form W-4**, Employee's Withholding Allowance Certificate, with your employer.

Caution: You may not make joint estimated tax payments if you or your spouse is a nonresident alien, you are separated under a decree of divorce or separate maintenance, or you and your spouse have different tax years.

Additional Information You May Need

Most of the information you will need can be found in:

Pub. 505, Tax Withholding and Estimated Tax

Other available information:

Pub. 553, Highlights of 1991 Tax Changes

Instructions for the 1991 Forms 1040 or 1040A

For forms and publications, call 1-800-829-3676

For assistance, call 1-800-829-1040

Tax Law Changes Effective for 1992

Use your 1991 tax return as a guide for figuring your estimated tax, but be sure to consider the changes noted in this section. For other changes that may affect your 1992 estimated tax, see Pub. 553.

Expiring Tax Provisions. At the time this package went to print, several tax provisions, including the self-employed health insurance deduction, were scheduled to expire 12/31/91. See Pub. 553 to find out if these provisions were extended.

Limit on Use of Prior Year's Tax. Some individuals (other than farmers and fishermen) with income over a certain amount must make a special computation to figure their estimated tax payments. Although these individuals may use 100% of their 1991 tax to figure the amount of their first payment, they may not be able to use that amount to figure their remaining payments. To see if this special computation applies to you, first fill in the 1992 Estimated Tax Worksheet (on page 3) through line 14b. Then, answer the questions below. But if you answer NO to any question, stop and read the instructions below question 3.

1. Did you make any estimated tax payments for 1991, 1990, or 1989, OR were you charged an estimated tax penalty for any of those years? (If either applies, answer "Yes.") . . . . ☐ Yes ☐ No

2. Is your 1992 adjusted gross income (AGI) on line 1 of the worksheet more than $75,000 ($37,500 if married filing separately)? . . . . ☐ Yes ☐ No

3. Do you expect your 1992 modified AGI (defined on page 2) to exceed your 1991 actual AGI by more than $40,000 ($20,000 if married filing separately)? . . . . . ☐ Yes ☐ No

If you answered NO to any of the questions above, you don't have to make the special computation. Instead, fill in the rest of the worksheet on page 3.

If you answered YES to all **three** of the questions above, you must make the special computation. Do not fill in the rest of the worksheet on page 3. Instead, use the 1992 **Estimated Tax Worksheet Limiting Use of Prior Year's Tax** in Pub. 505 to figure all your estimated tax payments. That worksheet uses 100% of your 1991 tax to figure your first payment.

Cat. No. 11340T

(Continued on page 2)

Department of the Treasury
Internal Revenue Service
Catalog Number 15154T

Publication 587

Business Use of Your Home

For use in preparing
1991 Returns

Declaration of Independence

When in the Course of human events it becomes necessary for one people to dissolve the political bands which have connected them with another, and to assume among the powers of the earth, the separate and equal station to which the Laws of Nature and of

Important Change

If you file a Schedule C, *Profit or Loss From Business,* with your Form 1040, you must use the new Form 8829, *Expenses for Business Use of Your Home,* to determine your deduction for business use of your home.

Important Reminders

If you use your home for business, you may be able to deduct some of your expenses for its business use. But you cannot deduct more than you receive in gross income from its business use.

If you are an employee or outside salesperson and the use of your home is an allowable business expense, you can generally deduct your unreimbursed expenses for using it as miscellaneous deductions on Schedule A (Form 1040). To figure how much you can deduct, total your unreimbursed expenses and subtract 2% of your adjusted gross income. This 2% limit on miscellaneous deductions does not apply to real estate taxes and deductible mortgage interest which are also deducted on Schedule A (Form 1040).

Introduction

You must meet specific tests to take a deduction for the business use of your home. Even if you meet these tests, your deduction is limited. This publication explains the requirements for taking the deduction. Use the worksheet at the end of this publication to help you figure the amount you can deduct. Some of the topics discussed are:

- Use Tests,
- Business Part of Home Expenses,
- What to Deduct,
- Deduction Limit,
- Where to Deduct,
- Day-Care Facility,
- Sale or Exchange of Your Home, and
- Business Furniture and Equipment.

The term *home* includes a house, apartment, condominium, mobile home, or boat. It also includes structures on the property, such as an unattached garage, studio, barn, or greenhouse. But it does not include any part of your property used exclusively as a hotel or inn.

Publication 534, *Depreciation,* will help you figure the amount of depreciation expense you can deduct for the business use of your home.

The publication is written for those who prepare their own returns. It does not discuss renting out your home, part of your home, or vacation property. For information about renting out your property, see Publication 527, *Residential Rental Property.*

The rules in this publication apply to individuals, trusts, estates, partnerships, and S corporations. They do not apply to corporations, other than S corporations. There are no special rules for the business use of a home by a partner or S corporation shareholder.

Free publications and forms. If you need information on a subject not covered in this publication, you may check our other free publications. To order publications and forms, call our toll-free telephone number 1–800–TAX–FORM (1–800–829–3676) or write the IRS Forms Distribution Center for your area as shown in the income tax package.

Use Tests

Whether you are an employee or self-employed, you generally cannot deduct expenses for the business use of your home. But you can take a

limited deduction for its business use if you meet the tests explained under the following discussions:

- Exclusive Use,
- Regular Use,
- Principal Place of Business,
- Place To Meet Patients, Clients, or Customers,
- Separate Structures, and
- Trade or Business Use.

To take a deduction for the use of part of your home, you must use that part *exclusively* and *regularly:*

1) As the principal place of business for any trade or business in which you engage,
2) As a place to meet or deal with patients, clients, or customers in the normal course of your trade or business, or
3) In connection with your trade or business, if you are using a separate structure that is not attached to your house or residence.

Employee use. Even if you meet the use tests, you cannot take any deduction based on the business use of your home if you are an employee and either of the following situations apply to you.

1) The business use of your home is not for the convenience of your employer. Whether your home's business use is for your employer's convenience depends on all the facts and circumstances. However, business use is not considered for your employer's convenience merely because it is appropriate and helpful.
2) You rent all or part of your home to your employer and use the rented portion to perform services as an employee.

Exclusive Use

"Exclusive use" means only for business. If you use part of your home as your business office and also use it for personal purposes, you do not meet the exclusive use test.

Example. You use a den in your home to write legal briefs and prepare tax returns. You also use the den for personal purposes. Therefore, you cannot claim a business deduction for using it.

Exceptions to Exclusive Use

There are two exceptions to the exclusive use test:

The use of part of your home for the storage of inventory, and
The use of part of your home as a day-care facility, discussed later under *Day-Care Facility.*

Storage of inventory. You can deduct expenses that relate to the use of part of your home for the storage of part of your home inventory, if you meet all of the following five tests.

1) The inventory must be kept for use in your trade or business.
2) Your trade or business must be the wholesale or retail selling of products.
3) Your home must be the only fixed location of your trade or business.
4) The storage space must be used on a regular basis.
5) The space used must be a separately identifiable space suitable for storage.

Example. Your home is the sole fixed location of your business of selling mechanics' tools at retail. You regularly use half of your basement for

SCHEDULE C
(Form 1040)

Department of the Treasury
Internal Revenue Service (O)

Profit or Loss From Business
(Sole Proprietorship)

▶ Partnerships, joint ventures, etc., must file Form 1065.

▶ Attach to Form 1040 or Form 1041. ▶ See Instructions for Schedule C (Form 1040).

OMB No. 1545-0074

1991

Attachment
Sequence No. 09

Name of proprietor	Social security number (SSN)

A	Principal business or profession, including product or service (see instructions)	B Enter principal business code (from page 2) ▶

C	Business name	D Employer ID number (Not SSN)

E   Business address (including suite or room no.) ▶ ....
    City, town or post office, state, and ZIP code

F   Accounting method: (1) ☐ Cash   (2) ☐ Accrual   (3) ☐ Other (specify) ▶ ....

G   Method(s) used to value closing inventory: (1) ☐ Cost (2) ☐ Lower of cost or market (3) ☐ Other (attach explanation) (4) ☐ Does not apply (if checked, skip line H) | Yes | No |

H   Was there any change in determining quantities, costs, or valuations between opening and closing inventory? (If "Yes," attach explanation) .

I   Did you "materially participate" in the operation of this business during 1991? (If "No," see instructions for limitations on losses.) . . .

J   If this is the first Schedule C filed for this business, check here . . . . ▶ ☐

Part I   Income

1	Gross receipts or sales. **Caution:** *If this income was reported to you on Form W-2 and the "Statutory employee" box on that form was checked, see the instructions and check here* ▶ ☐	1	
2	Returns and allowances	2	
3	Subtract line 2 from line 1	3	
4	Cost of goods sold (from line 40 on page 2)	4	
5	Subtract line 4 from line 3 and enter the gross profit here	5	
6	Other income, including Federal and state gasoline or fuel tax credit or refund (see instructions) .	6	
7	Add lines 5 and 6. This is your gross income. . . . . ▶	7	

Part II   Expenses (Caution: Enter expenses for business use of your home on line 30.)

8	Advertising	8		21	Repairs and maintenance .	21
9	Bad debts from sales or services (see instructions) .	9		22	Supplies (not included in Part III) .	22
10	Car and truck expenses (see instructions—also attach Form 4562) .	10		23	Taxes and licenses . .	23
11	Commissions and fees . .	11		24	Travel, meals, and entertainment:	
12	Depletion	12		a	Travel	24a
13	Depreciation and section 179 expense deduction (not included in Part III) (see instructions) .	13		b	Meals and entertainment	
14	Employee benefit programs (other than on line 19) .	14		c	Enter 20% of line 24b subject to limitations (see instructions)	
15	Insurance (other than health) .	15		d	Subtract line 24c from line 24b	24d
16	Interest:			25	Utilities	25
a	Mortgage (paid to banks, etc.) .	16a		26	Wages (less jobs credit) .	26
b	Other	16b		27a	Other expenses (list type and amount):	
17	Legal and professional services .	17			....	
18	Office expense . . .	18			....	
19	Pension and profit-sharing plans .	19			....	
20	Rent or lease (see instructions):				....	
a	Vehicles, machinery, and equipment	20a			....	
b	Other business property .	20b		27b	Total other expenses . .	27b

28	Add amounts in columns for lines 8 through 27b. These are your **total expenses** before expenses for business use of your home . . . . ▶	28	
29	Tentative profit (loss). Subtract line 28 from line 7	29	
30	Expenses for business use of your home (attach Form 8829)	30	
31	Net profit or (loss). Subtract line 30 from line 29. If a profit, enter here and on Form 1040, line 12. Also enter the net profit on Schedule SE, line 2 (statutory employees, see instructions). If a loss, you MUST go on to line 32 (fiduciaries, see instructions)	31	

32	If you have a loss, you MUST check the box that describes your investment in this activity (see instructions) .	32a ☐	All investment is at risk.
	If you checked 32a, enter the loss on Form 1040, line 12, and Schedule SE, line 2 (statutory employees, see instructions). If you checked 32b, you MUST attach Form 6198.	32b ☐	Some investment is not at risk.

For Paperwork Reduction Act Notice, see Form 1040 Instructions.   Cat. No. 11334P   Schedule C (Form 1040) 1991

Form **8829**	**Expenses for Business Use of Your Home**	OMB No. 1545-1256
	▶ File with Schedule C (Form 1040).	**1991**
Department of the Treasury Internal Revenue Service	▶ See instructions on back.	Attachment Sequence No. **66**
Name of proprietor		Your social security number

Part I — Part of Your Home Used for Business

1	Area used exclusively for business (see instructions). Include area used for inventory storage or as a day-care facility that does not meet exclusive use test	1	
2	Total area of home	2	
3	Divide line 1 by line 2. Enter the result as a percentage	3	%
	• For day-care facilities not used exclusively for business, also complete lines 4–6.		
	• All others, skip lines 4–6 and enter the amount from line 3 on line 7.		
4	Total hours facility used for day care during the year. Multiply days used by number of hours used per day	4	hr.
5	Total hours available for use during the year (365 days x 24 hours) (see instructions)	5	8,760 hr.
6	Divide line 4 by line 5. Enter the result as a decimal amount	6	
7	Business percentage. For day-care facilities not used exclusively for business, multiply line 6 by line 3 (enter the result as a percentage). All others, enter the amount from line 3 ▶	7	%

Part II — Figure Your Allowable Deduction

		(a) Direct expenses	(b) Indirect expenses	
8	Enter the amount from Schedule C, line 29. (If more than one place of business, see instructions.)			8
9	Casualty losses	9		
10	Deductible mortgage interest	10		
11	Real estate taxes	11		
12	Add lines 9, 10, and 11	12		
13	Multiply line 12, column (b) by line 7		13	
14	Add line 12, column (a) and line 13			14
15	Subtract line 14 from line 8. If zero or less, enter -0-			15
16	Excess mortgage interest (see instructions)	16		
17	Insurance	17		
18	Repairs and maintenance	18		
19	Utilities	19		
20	Other expenses	20		
21	Add lines 16 through 20	21		
22	Multiply line 21, column (b) by line 7		22	
23	Carryover of operating expenses from 1990		23	
24	Add line 21 in column (a), line 22, and line 23			24
25	Allowable operating expenses. Enter the **smaller** of line 15 or line 24			25
26	Limit on excess casualty losses and depreciation. Subtract line 25 from line 15			26
27	Excess casualty losses (see instructions)	27		
28	Depreciation of your home from Part III below	28		
29	Carryover of excess casualty losses and depreciation from 1990	29		
30	Add lines 27 through 29			30
31	Allowable excess casualty losses and depreciation. Enter the **smaller** of line 26 or line 30			31
32	Add lines 14, 25, and 31			32
33	Casualty losses included on lines 14 and 31. (Carry this amount to **Form 4684**, Section B.)			33
34	Allowable expenses for business use of your home. Subtract line 33 from line 32. Enter here and on Schedule C, line 30 ▶			34

Part III — Depreciation of Your Home

35	Enter the **smaller** of your home's adjusted basis or its fair market value (see instructions)	35	
36	Value of land included on line 35	36	
37	Basis of building. Subtract line 36 from line 35	37	
38	Business basis of building. Multiply line 37 by line 7	38	
39	Depreciation percentage (see instructions)	39	%
40	Depreciation allowable. Multiply line 38 by the percentage on line 39. Enter here and on line 28 above	40	

Part IV — Carryover of Unallowed Expenses to 1992

41	Operating expenses. Subtract line 25 from line 24. If less than zero, enter -0-	41	
42	Excess casualty losses and depreciation. Subtract line 31 from line 30. If less than zero, enter -0-	42	

For Paperwork Reduction Act Notice, see back of form.   Cat. No. 13232M   Form **8829** (1991)

How to Find Work,
Where to Get Help

Secret #225 It's the great gold rush of the '90s.

In bad economic times, finding consulting or freelance work is easier than ever. This is true, I believe, *because* millions of people have been laid off or fired or have taken early retirement.

Don't you know people who have been told to take a walk and not to bother to come back? (This happened to me, but it was exactly the kick in the pants that I needed to start my own business.)

Were they replaced?

Most were not, because payroll is the biggest expense of just about any company. Actual salaries represent only part of the expense. The killer for most employers is all those benefits, especially matching FICA and health insurance.

So who is doing all the work those millions of people used to do? In many cases, it's overworked staff people, and they're frustrated and tired and mad, and you can bet they are demanding help, in private, and at every staff meeting.

They need consultants and freelancers with many skills—people who proofread, do data processing, prepare reports, and do research; people who know how to work in a word-processing program, or in a graphics program, or who know how to transcribe tapes. They need writing help, art and design help, they need someone who knows how to put together a decent looking newsletter. They need an efficiency expert, they need to be organized, they need special events planned, lunch meetings catered, they need (fill in whatever it is you do here). Staff people are screaming for all kinds of help, and many of their big bosses may be listening.

Get on the phone, look in the paper, write letters, talk to people. There's gold out there, but you have to go find it.

HOT TIP: If you want to consult for large companies but aren't sure about what to charge, take the advice of Carolyn Karelitz, executive director of the Independent Computer Consultants Association in St. Louis. She advises new consultants to try to charge twice your hourly income that you were earning on a regular job. This is to cover insurance, overhead, and all those other goodies for which you now get to pay.

Secret #226 Why you have to do the undoable.

One thing has to be done nearly every day, or at a minimum, every week that you are in business, and it is at least as important as doing the work that you have promised to do.

You have to be looking for new work.

Weird as it may seem, no matter how high the work is piled up around your computer and strewn throughout the office, no matter how crazy you go trying to schedule everything, no matter how tired you are from the search, you have to return every call and follow each lead for new assignments, because you will eventually finish this pile, and then suddenly you may get a terrible surprise—there may be nothing to do. Which translates to no income next month.

This is possibly the greatest fear of anyone who runs a small business, that the work will stop coming in. Even if you have had a contract for years with your oldest, most trusted friend in the world who works for the most stable company anywhere, anything can happen. Your friend can have a heart attack and check out of this planet. That business can declare bankruptcy. A Democrat could get elected to be president. Hey, we're talking anything.

It's the type of thing that wakes you up at 3:57 A.M., and you lie there worrying about it for hours before finally falling down that sleep hole 17 seconds before the alarm goes off.

How do you go about finding new work when you're: (a) so busy with current work that you forget to make coffee, (b) so desperate for any work that you can't afford to make coffee, or (c) a Democratic hopeful?

You force yourself.

Secret #227 Yes, you can pull new work out of the air.

Many of the online services can be sources of freelance and full-time job opportunities. The possibility of making one good contact is worth the sign-up fee.

If you join CompuServe, for instance, you will receive a book that shows you all the destinations, or places, where you can find information. Under the "Industry and Professional Forums" section, you will see "Working from Home Forum." When you get into it, there are messages from all around the country, which are memos that people type to you and everybody else. (If you never get any mail, this could be a huge ego booster for you: "Heard from a friend in Juneau, Alaska," you could say, or "Got a note from a guy in San Diego.")

A typical listing could look like this:

SUBJ: Blah company, NY   Section: Work at home
From: J. Workmeister   (ID numbers here)
To: All   Date: Today

Opportunities exist for many people to be hired to do exactly whatever it is that you enjoy doing the most during your working hours. We will pay your top salary tripled if you will work with us from your home starting anytime after noon and finishing before 4 P.M. Please contact_____. Thank you!

Not all entries will look exactly like this one, but you get the point. If you have a printer, you can download, or print out a copy of these listings on paper.

Whether you find work the electronic way, or open up the phone book and start calling people, or hire kids to slip flyers about your service onto front doors of homes and shops, you will find work, if you try. The main thing is to let the right people know that you can do what they need to have done, at the right price.

Secret #228   The bucks stopped there.

As anyone knows who has been in business for more than five minutes, times have a way of getting bad. It begins to show up in subtle ways.

Like eight-inch-high headlines on your paper's front page—"Nation Enters Recession." You hear that guy's voice, the one who reads all the stock report figures on every radio station everywhere, saying "Leading economic indicators all point to a slowdown . . . " while you keep looking for some good station. And here's the very same guy saying, "Prices on Wall Street took a nose dive again today . . . "

So what if stupid Wall Street has gone off the deep end again, you think. I haven't invested every penny I own and could borrow in stock, you think. How could that possibly affect me and my business?

How it could possibly affect you is that companies hear this same news and tighten their belts and don't spend money for a while, creating that famous trickle-down effect you hear so much about. Your phone doesn't ring. There is no work. The spending slowdown is at your front door.

What do people who run small businesses do to hold on during times like this?

What you don't want to do is lose your wits and go all crazy on us and rant about how you should never have done this. Save that reaction for the times you are so busy, you can't find time to hyperventilate. Now here's the game plan.

Secret #229   Love the ones
you're with.

The thing is, if your small business is suffering, think
about all the medium and large companies that are sweating
it out, too. One of the few good things about bad times is
that it's equally hard on just about everybody. So consider
yourself pretty lucky if any clients are spending money
right now.

Work your hardest to please the clients who are sticking
with you during the lean times. They'll think twice about
using another company if you are giving them much better
service than they could get anywhere else.

Offer a better deal, discounts, specials, or free additional
service with the regular package. If you're a consultant,
throw in a few free hours of your time, if there is a need
for this. You can't lose, and the client sees that you have
that extra dedication that every employer wishes they got
from their staff members.

Of course, this extra dedication is directly due to the fact
that you like to eat, but don't be obvious about it.

Some experts advise that you focus on increasing every
current project or job rather than going after new customers.
Take the money you might have spent on ads or direct mail,
and use it to let the clients working with you know that
they're getting a good deal.

About two to three weeks after you've done the work,
call the client and ask how is it going, were they satisfied
with the job, do they need anything else from you to make
it perfect. Force yourself not to ask about your check. This
is not the purpose of this call.

"Wrap a warm blanket" around all your valued customers or clients during the bad times, advises writer Bob Bly,

a marketing consultant in New Jersey who published a 16-page booklet called *Special Report* about marketing in an economic downturn.*

Nearly all business owners agree that you should not immediately lower your prices during a downturn, although if you need to do something drastic to hold onto clients who may be shopping around, this may be what you have to do.

Above all—be optimistic and even encouraging to others. It's contagious, and it doesn't cost you a cent.

*To order a copy of Bly's *Special Report,* write to him at 174 Holland Ave., New Milford, N.J., 07646.

Secret #230 Spend it to make it.

If you are convinced that the best thing to do during a slump is to spend money and aggressively go after new accounts, you have a lot of other experts agreeing with you on this. Small business owners have done everything you can think of to land new work. They've joined local networking groups to make new contacts, made cold calls in an ice age of a market, bought major pieces of new equipment to one-up competitors, and worked out deals with other types of businesses to offer expanded services, even to the point of joining forces with competitors, renaming these mergers "strategic alliances" instead of using the older phrase "let's see what happens when we put two starving lions in the same cage together."

Ad people say that this is the most critical time for increasing your advertising budget (what an odd thing for ad people to say). Marketing consultants suggest that you revamp your image, that the perfect time to have your logo redesigned and new stationery printed is when times are lean, especially if this was something that you had done very quickly in your early days and you're not totally satisfied with it. (Yeah right, like who can afford these designers even in good times.)

For those professionals who rely on word of mouth to build their practice, such as doctors, lawyers, accountants, and hookers, consultants suggest they send out newsletters or give seminars to project a sense of professional expertise and build up a more positive image.

Secret #231 Or save it to keep it.

If you have no money to spend on fancy-dancy equipment during the lean times, if you in fact hardly have enough to pay your own salary, then you are in with an enormously large group of people known as the American small business community.

All small businesses that are alive today owe their success in staying alive, in part, to the same old-fashioned values that saw our nation through its worst depression during the 1930s. It may sound funny and unhip today, but being frugal, making cost decisions carefully, and trimming your expenses as much as possible is a proven way to hang on.

If your business is in your home, I believe that you have the best chance to tough it out longer than others. If you want to rent office space, consider a flexible lease arrangement called shared office space, or executive suites. This deal allows you to rent the square footage that you need, along with such goodies as the use of equipment and conference rooms, and services that probably include a receptionist to cover phones and perhaps an office manager. The beauty of this is that if your business drops off, you can scale back the amount of square footage and expenses to half or one-third. The trick is to keep your clients from knowing about it, which can damage your credibility.

Some people who have really been hit hard have even moved their offices out entirely, but have still maintained that executive identity by having the phone answered in their company's name, while continuing to use the conference rooms and equipment.

Another cost-cutting idea is using temporary help instead of hiring full-time employees, if your business can work this way. Every workday, about one million temps are sent out to companies of all sizes to answer phones, work on the computer, assemble products, update mailing lists, and do special projects (*The Washington Post,* February 18, 1991). They're not cheap, but it's an on-call service for which you only pay a certain number of hours, and your small business budget doesn't get hit with matching FICA or benefits, those twin killer expenses.

HOT TIP: You can get a free booklet called *How to Buy Temporary Help Services* by sending a stamped, self-addressed envelope to National Association of Temporary Services, 119 S. St. Asaph St., Alexandria, VA 22314.

Secret #232 Where to go when the banks say no.

Your small, stable business has a good credit rating, is an excellent risk, and needs a business loan that you'll guarantee personally. No one has better credit than you, and yet at least two banks have said no.

This is great!

This means that you are now qualified to apply for a loan guaranteed by the Small Business Administration (SBA). These loans used to be considered a last resort for high-risk borrowers, but they have become the darling of bankers across the country, according to an administrator for the SBA in D.C. Nationally, 93% of all SBA-guaranteed loans are current and performing, a figure that bankers just love. To find out which banks in your area make loans to small businesses, call your local SBA office, or the U.S. SBA's Small Business Answer Desk. Their toll-free number is 1-800/827-5722*.

You'll get a recording that tells you about starting a small business, where to find financing, information about SCORE, which is the Service Corps of Retired Executives (more about this wonderful group of people coming right up), types of ownership, such as sole proprietorship, incorporation, or partnership, publications you can request, local assistance (here you have to enter your area code), and more business data.

If you call from 9 A.M. to 5 P.M. EST, Monday through

*The number for the SBA, if you don't want to go through the Small Business Answer Desk, is 202/205-6600. Don't tell them I told you—they have enough to do without my plastering their direct line all across America.

Friday, you'll eventually get to speak with a real live person who will try to answer your specific questions. Keep in mind that this answer desk received over a quarter of a million calls in 1989, which is more phone calls than three popular teenage girls *combined* get in one year. The staff is friendly and helpful, and they'll try to refer you to your local SBA office or another place where you can get free or low-cost help.

The SBA has more information to help you and more money earmarked for women, in particular, than ever before, due to the fact that businesses owned by women are the fastest growing part of the small business community. Every SBA district office in the nation has a women's business ownership representative who is responsible for increasing awareness of SBA's programs and for helping prospective businesswomen who come to the SBA.

One of the many steps you will take will be learning to prepare a business plan. Whoa—what's this? Why do I need a business plan, you may be asking.

If you can start on a shoestring, they are a waste of paper and time. If you need to get a loan to start up, however, you're going to have to do what the banks want, and billions of bankers who look like that little guy in the top hat on a Monopoly board want to see your plan on paper. That's just the way they operate.

The SBA probably won't lend you the money, but what they will do is guarantee your loan (90% guarantee up to $150,000 that you borrow, 85% guarantee for amounts between $150,000 and $750,000) to a bank that will lend it to you, if the SBA believes that: (a) you have no other way to get financing; (b) that you can make your business work; (c) and that you will pay back the money.

Now all you have to do is convince the SBA of these facts. Hey, cherie, compared to what you are getting into, this is The Big Easy.

Secret #233 Lots of ways to spell HELP.

Small Business Development Centers (SBDCs).

If you are just starting out, the SBA will probably suggest you call your local Small Business Development Center. Forty-four states have SBDCs at or near their state universities. These centers offer courses on starting and running a small business, and they focus on start-ups and businesses in early stages. Contact your state university, or the SBA's answer desk at 1-800/368-5855. Or you can send $1.00 for a booklet, *The Business Plan for Home-Based Businesses,* to:

> SBA Publications
> P.O. Box 30
> Denver, CO 80201-0030

Small Business Institutes (SBIs)

Also located at colleges and universities and funded through the SBA. If you are an established business, these SBIs will consult with you on market surveys, new product analyses, and other areas in which you may need help. Contact your local college or university for more information.

Office of Women's Business Ownership

Also part of the SBA. Offers counseling and support for women business owners and entrepreneurs. Their address:

1441 L St., N.W., Suite 414
Washington, DC 20416
Phone: 202/653-8000

Economic Development Administration (EDA)

This is part of the U.S. Department of Commerce, which sponsors research and development centers all across the nation. They provide help and assistance in the areas of management and technical advice, along with developing loan packages and help in the search for capital, to small business owners of all sexes.

Their hotline: 1-800/424-5197.

American Woman's Economic Development Center (AWED)

Offers counseling programs to assist women entrepreneurs, including seminars on business management, consultation for how to obtain loans, specialized assistance, advice, pats on the back. Their address:

60 East 42nd St., Suite 405
New York, NY 10165
Phone: 212/692-9100

Office of Minority Business Enterprise (OMBE)

Sponsored by the U.S. Department of Commerce, this group funds hundreds of regional business development offices across the country. They hold conferences for minority women in business, and they provide advice in management, training, and technical services. Address:

U.S. Department of Commerce
Washington, D.C. 20230
Phone: 202/377-2000

Additionally, there are thousands of networks and groups throughout America that are standing by, ready to help you. Call local banks and accounting firms and ask if they have any free information they could send you about starting a small business. Check the business calender in your local paper for the location, date, and time of meetings sponsored by groups of entrepreneurs. Talk to other business people, check your library, keep your ears and eyes open. There's a whole lot going on.

Secret #234 Wait—before you call that $250/hour consultant, call SCORE!

Of the small businesses that fail—and according to what you read, that figure is anywhere from 33% to 87%—the two things that kill most of them are poor management and lack of finance, according to Bob Leavitt, the Washington D.C. area chairman of SCORE (which, as you know, stands for Service Corps of Retired Executives).

Fortunately for small business owners like you and me, the SBA can lend its powerful muscle with the first and its awesome financial resources with the second.

The trick is to get through their ever-busy telephone lines and schedule some consulting time with a volunteer.

If you can get an appointment with one of the SCORE volunteer counselors, you'll tap into a major source of solid, credible advice for your small business.

First of all, they're not your Aunt JoHelen who knows nothing about running a business but would love to give you her opinion. These men and women have been through just about everything in the business world, having come from long careers at companies of all sizes. They've volunteered their time, which says something about their dedication. They know how to identify your weak points, and they can advise you on how to emphasize your strong skills. And their services are practically free.

A business in trouble can be helped by a SCORE SWAT team that moves in, formulating and directing plans to help.

If you feel you need to get financial help, they'll warn you to be ready to explain to a banker why you need a loan, as well as help you with the other preparation and paperwork involved. If you want advice about which method is best for your business, whether you should form a sole proprietorship or become incorporated, and what is involved with a legal partnership, they can help you with all that good stuff. If your service or product is great, but you need to beef up your marketing, they're going to tell you.

It's up to you to make the ultimate decisions and carry them out, but that's because you're lucky enough to be the boss.

Secret #235 Wait—before you call that $500/hour attorney, call the small business legal clinic of your local university.

Imagine walking onto the campus of a respected, elite school, such as George Washington University in Washington, D.C., and going into the Law School, where you find a Small Business Legal Clinic abuzz with third-year law students who are ready to help you set up your new small business—for less than the cost of dinner for two.

This actually is available to people like you and me. I know because I've gone there several times and talked with Dan Gropper, the energetic, upbeat attorney who used to head the clinic, and the bright young men and women who practice there. I only wish I'd known about this group back in 1982 when we paid about 20 times more money to a fancy-pants downtown law firm for the exact same paperwork.

For your minuscule investment, the people who work at these legal clinics will go through all the machinations with you—show you how to file for your Federal Employer ID number, how to obtain permits and licenses, how to incorporate, and what papers you need to fill out—plus they'll give you all kinds of good advice. (You have to pay for permits, filing fees, and other outside costs, but these usually are extremely low, too.)

GWU is just one of many universities and colleges that small business owners can go to for low-cost help and legal guidance. Call your local schools and ask what they offer.

You never know what's out there until you ask.

Secret #236   Fear of failure.

When you think about it, everyone else should be worried, not you. If all those people driving along in their cars to their jobs were to realize how easy it is to get fired today, or how quickly any company can go under and everybody could lose their jobs, they'd be blithering, dribbling messes, more commonly referred to as vice-presidents.

As your own boss, you have taken matters into your hands. By grabbing the helm and being independent, you have eliminated 99% of the reasons for anyone else causing you to fall down.

On your own, you get to call the shots, not the CEO or the COO or the president or any of the COO-COOs upstairs.

You are strong. In fact, with your winning attitude and ability to do unlimited hard work, you are practically invincible, especially during a recession, when small businesses that are not heavily in debt have the tenacity of Velcro, picking up lots of spillover work from places that have been forced to tell other, more expensive companies and contractors to take a hike.

Now I'm not going to try to tell you that you won't ever be afraid of failure, or give you some greeting card line like "The only thing that can cause you to fail is your attitude," or something like that (even though it's true). I can't promise you that you won't wake up in a cold sweat after 10 months or 10 years, worried about the health of your small business.

But here is a suggestion for how to handle this. Set aside a time, such as between 2:30 A.M. and 3:30 A.M. every other Tuesday, to worry about failure. Every time you start to think about how you might have made the most humongous mistake of your life, remind yourself that you'll think about it during your worry hour next Tuesday. Then sleep through it.

Secret #237 The real odds on succeeding.

We're all making it up as we go along. There aren't any rules anywhere. Running your own business is like playing poker and the dog has eaten one card out of each suit. At any moment, the entire bottom could cave in and everybody would fall all the way through to China, where most of us would pick ourselves up, brush off the dust, and start another small business.

You have to be looney tunes to want to do this.

This is one of the reasons why I genuinely like other small business owners, why I feel an enormous affiliation with them, why I enjoy talking with them and hearing their stories. We've all been through the same thing, veterans with this experience in common.

Why do we keep doing it?

I can't speak for you, but I don't like the alternatives.

Plus there's always the chance that someone will benefit in some way from your work.

Woody Allen put it so well in an interview: "If my film makes one more person feel miserable, I'll feel I've done my job."

Service:
Good, Better, Best.
Then There Is Yours

Secret #238 It's my turn.

Has this ever happened to you?

You've been waiting in line in a department store to pay for something, and the line inches up slowly, and finally, after a century, it's your turn.

The phone on the desk rings.

The salesperson answers it and talks to the caller!

Doesn't this kill you? Whether you realize it or not, someone cut in front of you in line and got away with it.

You can also experience this rudeness when you are sitting in your client's office and she/he takes a call, and suddenly you are invisible while they discuss the office retreat for twenty-seven minutes.

Your time matters, if not to anyone else, at least to you—unless, of course, there is nothing else that you could be doing right now, in which case you are an impostor and not running your own business. There's always something else you could be doing when you're running a business.

Remember this feeling when you're having a meeting with someone who works with you or who is doing a freelance project for you. Don't leap up and grab the phone just because it is ringing, demanding to be answered.

If you can't have someone else answer it for a while, then put it on call forwarding to your answering service, or turn the answering machine on, or (GASP!) take the lamebrain thing off the hook for a few minutes. Not that I've ever done this, but let's just say I've heard of it being done.

The telephone, as wonderful as it can be, can also be one of the greatest intrusions ever devised since snoopy little brothers who find the key and look into your diary. Just because you can't see the person or the computer calling doesn't mean it's less rude to the person trying to talk with you. It is exactly the same as if someone else plopped into your lap and started talking to you, and you forgot the other person was there.

It's called respect, and Aretha Franklin spelled it the best.

Secret #239 You have to be your toughest competitor.

Every time you do a new job for a client, it has to be the best you can do. If you're lucky enough to have a regular, ongoing project, such as a publication or a contract for providing services, it always has to be as good as the time before, or better. There is no getting around this, if you want to maintain your terrific, hard-earned image of giving great service.

The idea of giving good service to clients is on the rise again after being in a freefall for years, thanks to factors including major economic upheaval, deregulation, the concept of self-service in every facet of American life, and the general "I don't give a flying fig" attitude that started with James Dean in the movie *Rebel without a Good Business Approach*.

Time did a cover article (February 2, 1987) titled "Why Is Service So Bad?" In that article, the writer quoted Thomas Peters, coauthor of *In Search of Excellence,* as saying "in general, service in America stinks." It was predicted that "quality of service" was on its way to becoming the next business buzz phrase, and there's plenty of evidence that this is exactly what happened, since American companies always need a new buzz thing to keep them hopping.

In the corporate shakeout years that followed, businesses of all types and sizes went under, but many that made it mandatory for their employees to think of good service as their number one priority have held on.

Nordstrom, the Seattle-based department store chain, has one rule for every employee—the customer has to leave satisfied. Looks like somebody in Nordstrom's top management watched *Miracle on 34th Street* where Macy's went so far as to recommend their shoppers go to Gimbel's, which made everyone want to come to Macy's.

Author Ron Zemke, in his book *The Service Edge,* describes 101 American companies whose success is attributed to giving great service. He mentions L.L. Bean, where employees are trained for a week before they ever talk to a customer on the phone. L.L. Bean is great—how many other companies can you call up and order something from their catalog on Christmas Eve and have it delivered the next day? This is service.

Not that you want your clients to ask you to do anything on Christmas Eve, but you want to let them think that you could handle special requests because you value their business. You must be willing to make them feel as though they're getting the best service that money can buy.

This whole idea of giving great service is not new. One of the special services we offer to our clients is deluxe proofreading by Aida Pirk, our four-level proofreader.

It's odd, I can proof a page that was also proofed by the client, and we both miss a plural or don't catch a transposed word. But Aida does, every time. Service like this could be one reason why women-owned businesses are the fastest-growing sector of the American economy, according to the Small Business Administration, as well as having higher sales volume and profits than male-owned businesses, according to the Census Bureau, which also says that women-owned firms jumped up 57% from 1982 to 1987.

But you don't have to be a woman to give good service or to get mentioned by the SBA. All you have to do is work your complete tail off.

Proof those extra pages, even if it's late and you're tired.

Send the stuff out to Utah by fax to get it approved by the right person.

Identify the people in the photos, and spell their names right.

Check the finished product two or three times.

Add up the columns.

Figure out the puzzles, check to see that it all makes sense.

Paying attention to the smallest details, as well as getting the big things right, will make all the difference in the world to your client.

It's not easy to think of everything, but you can learn to do it. The more you do it, the better you get. The better you get, the more your client is dependent on you and only you to get it right the first time. The more dependent your client is on you, the longer your business is going to be around.

Secret #240 "I think one of your couriers sideswiped my car."

Our neighbor called and said this to me one day. This is not the type of problem you want to have when you run a small business out of your home on a quiet, peaceful street, where your image should be at least 30% more positive than that of the Good Samaritan.

We immediately took the phones off the hook (for the first time in our agency's history, of course) and went across the street to survey the damage.

Sure enough, her car had been scraped along the driver's side, right where our couriers pull out of the alley after dropping off a package or making a pickup, usually in a roadrunner-type hurry. Now as far as dress code is concerned, you might not want any of them to escort you to a White House state dinner, but as drivers, most of them are as skillful as they are quick.

As we explained to our neighbor, it was hard to believe that any of these people would risk trying to get by with doing something like this, because it would definitely cause problems for the company and the driver if it were proven.

She was sure that this was what had happened, however, since her car was right in the line of fire, and couriers had been in and out that morning. We talked for a while on her front porch, finally deciding that we would call the owner of the courier company and ask them to pay for it, and if they wouldn't, that we would cover it. This is what you have to do sometimes, I believe, to maintain your good image. We walked toward the street to go back to work.

And then a miracle happened.

Her friend pulled up in a big station wagon, double-parked, and got out of the car, red-faced, apologizing, and tripping all over herself. She had been there earlier to drop off something, in a terrific hurry, and she had accidentally scraped the side of our neighbor's car and did not have the time to go inside to tell her, and she was so sorry, and of course she would pay for it, and blah-blah-blah.

We haven't had one complaint since then.

Secret #241 Does that come in gold glitter?

When you're in the service business, there will be times that you will be called upon to perform miracles, so have your little miracle wand handy at all times. (Page 102 of the Amazing Stuff catalog, $99.95 each.)

In our case, it was the client's printer who said, "We're ready to go on press and we can't use the artwork that you produced," and we could hear the big printing presses gearing up in the background, waiting for clearance to take off.

Could we get new artwork together and taken to Federal Express before 8:30 P.M. that night so the printer could get it first thing the next morning? Sure, I said, half of me calm while the other half frantically called the service bureau on another phone, knowing that the entire account was at stake.

No problem, said David at the service bureau 20 miles away. This won't take long. You guys can do an electronic transmission via the modem, and we'll produce what you need, he said.

Except their equipment jammed.

Then it jammed again. And again. (David later said that on a job as important as this, the equipment somehow senses what's going on and will jam up. Or it will run out of film entirely. Or the electricity will fail in their neighborhood.) At some point, another person, Maria, became involved, promising us that as soon as the artwork was ready, she would handcarry it over to the Federal Express office a mile away and make sure the package got out that night.

We paced, unable to eat or drink anything, not knowing

what was going to happen, looking at the phone in quiet desperation, afraid to call, afraid to not call.

Finally at 8:26 P.M., the artwork was ready. David and Maria grabbed it and raced down to the Fed Ex office, arriving there at 8:32 P.M.

Locked up tight.

Maria knocked on the door, begging with the guy inside to *please* take this package.

He'd seen this before. Hardened by all the emergencies that happen every day, knowing he'd probably be there all night unless he locked up when the clock hit 8:30, he motioned for her to drop it in the night box.

She had a feeling that meant it would not get processed and delivered that night, so she begged some more.

No dice.

(Keep in mind that we did not know David and Maria any better than you do, except that we had spoken with them by phone and knew them to be hardworking and dependable. But this type of service from them was unbelievable.)

So they took their miserable package and went back to the service bureau. At this point, I would have said that they had definitely given it their best shot. In the meantime, I had been calling the airlines, and Kathy and I were prepared to drive the package to our airport at 5:30 A.M. to get it on a dawn departure to Indianapolis, the nearest big city to the printer. If necessary, I was going to fly it there myself, rent a car, and drive the package to the printer 30 miles away.

Instead of calling us in defeat, however, Maria contacted Sky Courier, a delivery service that picked up the package at midnight and took it to the airport, where someone put it on the next flight out, and it was met on the other end by a courier who drove it straight to the print shop.

Thanks to David, Maria, and Sky Courier, we met the deadline and kept the account. We sent a warm letter about David and Maria to the president of their company, as well as a small bonus check to each of them for a job well done.

Why is it that some people will go to these lengths without even being asked, and others will give up before 8:30? I don't know.

But I do know that sometimes you get as good as you give.

Secret #242 It's on your nickel.

Ah, the telephone.

Some people wear earrings; I have an ivory-colored handset growing out of my left ear.

But when you run a small business, you can't do without it. And the communications companies are always adding new options for us, such as the toll-free 800 number.

The major companies have identified three potentially huge markets for this service: truckers and other occupational travelers, children who talk with elderly parents long distance, and people who are working out of their homes.

If your prospective clients can call you long distance and not have to pay for the call, this could definitely enhance your image, put you ahead of your competitors, and might be worth checking out, unless you're afraid your in-laws in Biloxi would get the number and call you all the time.

AT&T offers a Starterline 800 service for small, home-based businesses that receive less than three hours of toll-free calls in a month. MCI has a Personal 800 service, and Sprint brings us the Residential 800, both of which are tied in to regular home phones, but I won't tell them you use it for your small business if you don't tell them.

Try to get in during one of the special times, such as when a company is offering free installation. You don't have to buy the 800 service from your current long distance carrier. You can buy it from any of them. This is America.

A partner in the Manhattan office of one of the Big Eight accounting firms says, "The beauty of having an 800 number is that when someone calls, you are talking to a hot prospect. Even if the call costs you a dollar, it's not a lot to spend."

As for outbound, long distance calls, you can buy minutes or time in bulk, just like dog food and detergent.

Small companies known as aggregators buy blocks of long-distance minutes from AT&T, then turn around and resell the minutes to businesses of all sizes, offering discounts depending on the number of calls you make.

Telecommunications consultants say that if your company spends $100 or more per month on long-distance calls, you might be better off buying blocks of time.

Secret #243   This one's for you.

Offer yourself a good service once in a while, too. Consider giving the office a whole new look. You don't have to be earning the interest from a million-dollar trust fund to be able to afford to lift your spirits.

Have beautiful wall-to-wall carpet installed, give the walls a new paint job, install miniblinds, buy some new pieces of furniture, or maybe hang up some nice artwork or prints on the walls, or something special that your six-year-old daughter created. You would be amazed at the difference this can make in your attitude about going to work in your office, especially if it used to be the dingy old family room in your home.

Secret #244 This one's for your vendors.

A few years ago, one of the largest, most influential advertising agencies in the D.C. area called all of its employees into a meeting right after 5 P.M. and told them the agency had just declared Chapter 7 bankruptcy and had closed its doors, for good.

This does wonders for employee morale, as you can imagine. Not only did these people suddenly not have jobs, but also several print shops, type houses, television and radio stations, and hundreds of outside vendors including artists, writers, and media people suddenly acquired bad debts on their books.

One printer was owed over a quarter of a million dollars by this agency, and as far as I know, they never saw any of it. Another printer, burned by this same agency and already troubled by slow payments or non-payments from other places, sent out a letter to every one of its customers, gently demanding that the customer personally guarantee payment in the event that their company went under, and asked that the form be notarized. If you didn't sign and notarize it, they would only do business on a COD basis.

Although several business people who had been using this printer for years were upset about the notarized letter bit, I didn't blame the printer at all. They were protecting their assets.

Even though this might be a tough thing for a business person to do, you should guarantee to all your vendors that they will be paid, whether you get paid by your clients or not. Just having this as a policy and letting the right people know about it can enhance your image immeasurably.

But you have to be willing to back it up, if necessary. Borrow from your AMEX Gold Card, cash in your bonds, get tough on the people who owe you. But pay your vendors.

Secret #245 Types of people to avoid.

1. Anyone who keeps you waiting longer than a half hour for a meeting, unless it's your ob-gyn delivering a baby, which they'd better name after you.

2. People who keep you waiting, and when they finally meet you, they actually blurt out that they forgot you were waiting for them, which was why you had to wait longer. (Yes, this has happened to us.)

3. People who work in computer software firms who are so busy every single minute that they barely have time to meet with you and thentheyhavetosqueezeinyour meetingbetweencalls.

4. People who work in any field who are as busy as the jerks in number 3.

5. People who leer lecherously at you, tell you that you look like their cousin in New York, and ask you if you're sure that the two of you haven't met somewhere before.

6. People who keep you waiting, and when you finally do meet them, you have this terrible feeling in your gut that you shouldn't have come to this meeting and you want to leave. Know what you should do? Leave. Right then. Act like you're an identical twin and you just had an incredible vision that your other half needs you immediately on the other side of the continent. Say anything—just follow your gut and get out of there.

7. People above the age of eight who greet you with hand buzzers and other practical jokes.

8. People who are totally devoid of a sense of humor. I've found, over the years, that this one quality means more than all the others put together.

Secret #246 Let your fingers do the flying.

Overnight door-to-door pickup and delivery services rank right up there with the coffee and danish cart as one of the best things to happen to businesses of all sizes. Federal Express has a toll-free 800 number answered by a pleasant computer voice which, when you call from a push-button phone and punch in your account number, zip code, and number of packages at your pickup location, will give you back a confirmation number. You can get a real person if you stay on the line, or if you call from a rotary dial telephone.

Federal Express has plenty of competitors, including Airborne, UPS, DHL, Sky Courier, Emery, Greyhound, every major airline, Amtrak, and even the good old U.S. Postal Service with its Overnight Letters.

We've used most of these at some point, and they're all customer-oriented, dependable services, but my hands-down favorite is Federal Express. They've streamlined the procedure, making it as easy as possible to use by sending out tons of free, imprinted forms and supplies on request, designing their form so it's easy to fill out, and always, always, always getting the package there, even when I have screwed up.

We stopped at a McDonald's for coffee, somewhere on the road between Rehoboth Beach, Delaware, and a small town in Indiana. My mind wasn't really on work, since we had taken off for a much deserved week's vacation, but on a whim I called the answering service, just to see which of our clients might have left a funny message, like telling us they got a new agency.

The tone was ominous. We'd had several urgent messages during the last 24 hours to call Mr. Jennings at his office *immediately*. Mr. Jennings was our newest, biggest, most important account at the time.

I called Mr. Jennings. Before leaving town, we'd wrapped up several projects for him, shipping some time-sensitive ads out by Federal Express to California.

One ad had never arrived, and the publisher in Long Beach was screaming that he had to go to print *today*. There was no time to produce a new one and get it out to the West Coast in time, even if we'd been in our office, which we were nowhere near.

Someone in the central office of Federal Express connected me to the Los Angeles office, which patched me through to the courier in his van on one of the L.A. freeways, who went through his log and persisted until he found the package sitting in a local Federal Express office, waiting to be picked up.

As it turned out, I had checked the wrong box on the form, the box that means someone will call for it rather than to deliver it to an address.

YIKES! Talk about embarrassed. And talk about grateful.

The courier drove it directly over to the publisher in Long Beach, and the ad was there in time to go to press with the rest of the book. I thanked the courier profusely, and I thanked the people in the L.A. office profusely, and I thanked the people in the central office profusely, and then I wrote a letter to the president of Federal Express, thanking him profusely for having such great people who go the distance and for their responsiveness and level of service and for saving our account.

Federal Express Corporation sent us a certificate for a free overnight letter to anywhere, and of course Mr. Jennings' account got that certificate along with my profuse apology, at which point Mr. Jennings, in his inimitable style, told me to stop being so profuse about every stupid thing, that it wasn't life or death, for crying out loud.

Secret #247 The Stepford phones.

There is a new kind of corporate terrorism in the business world. It's called voice mail, and you are the hostage.

You've probably called somewhere and had a computer answer the phone:

"Welcome to Marshmallow Puff Land. If you know your party's direct line, enter the four-digit extension now."

(Which you don't.)

The computer continues. "If you want information about what is actually in marshmallow puff cookies, enter 1 now and press the star code."

(You keep waiting, because you have all the time in the world.)

"If you want to know what the proper beverage is to serve with marshmallow puff cookies, enter 2 now, press the pound code, followed by the star code, then your party's four-digit extension which you don't know, so why not hang up now."

(Could you possibly have heard correctly?)

"If you want to find out what sizes marshmallow puff cookies come in, enter 3 now, followed by the alto part of 'The Battle Hymn of the Republic' and just see if you get through, you old rat bag."

If, somewhere along this route, you happen to accidentally enter some person's actual four-digit extension while spelling out in four letters what you think about this company's voice mail system, you won't get a person, but you'll probably hear something like this:

"The party you are trying to reach ... " (and then there's this coffin-like voice inserting a name like Binkie Radabaugh, only it sounds like iowhhnk whebklbk) "is not at her desk or is in a meeting at this time. If you would like to leave a message, wait for the tone. When you are finished, press that tic-tac-toe sign, you stupid hunk of concrete. To review your message, press your secret PIN and account numbers at all your banks. To change your message, press in Julio Iglesias's private phone number in Malta.''

By now you may have guessed that I have had some problems with voice mail systems.

Didn't you know we were in trouble when people started getting answering machines at home? Having a machine answer your phone at home is one thing, but I think we crossed some kind of invisible line when we started thinking this might be a good idea at the office.

Funny thing is, those $99.95 home answering machines are often better quality than billion-dollar voice mail systems.

My personal theory about the use of voice mail is that they have killed off all the people who work in those offices and replaced them with Stepford-type personnel. This is the only possible explanation as to why formerly nice companies would suddenly do this to us.

There are other ideas about why voice mail exists. Certain influential columnists who call Fortune 500 companies a lot believe that these systems say a lot about the organizations that use them, that while they may be a marvelous tool for the organization, they can indicate a total contempt for anyone outside. In fact, the number one reason most companies purchase these systems is not to make it easier for anyone to call the company, but to lower the cost and increase the efficiency of intra-company communications.

Sociologist James E. Katz, who studies the human impact of telecommunication systems for Bellcore, a research arm of the Bell operating companies, stated that he thinks "it's regrettable that so many organizations fail to adequately consider the needs of the customers when they install these systems. They mainly consider the internal need of the company so outsiders get turned off to the experience when they call in and try to talk to some-one.''(*The Washington Post*, October 19, 1990).

Langdon Winner of Rensselaer Polytechnic and author of *Autonomous Technology*, which is an influential critique of innovations in the wonderful world of technology, has another theory about voice mail. He writes, ''What we're seeing is the hollowing of the organizational social system. Instead of complementing the way people communicate in organizations, the technology is designed to replace it.'' He goes on to write that in this different kind of social system, people would rather transfer you to the technology than deal with you directly, because this is the value that the company is trying to reinforce.

To be fair, they're not all bad—maybe just 95% of them. I have to call a lot of places, and in a way, it's sometimes a relief not to have to talk to a real person. It's easier some-times just to leave a message. Then the ball is in their court.

But you do get the feeling, after dialing enough of these places, that a lot of people in corporate la-la land don't want to talk with anyone, that in their minds, you're noth-ing more than a data entry device.

And sooner or later, all the real people out here are going to get the message.

Secret #248 Can you hold on a second? I have to pull the rip cord to my parachute.

Results from a recent survey indicate that an overwhelming percentage of Americans—some 792%—agree that anyone who uses a car phone or a car fax machine or a car copier or any other piece of office equipment in their car while driving should be nuked.

Really—what is this obsession that some people have with working in their car *while driving?* Most of us wouldn't mind (according to this extremely scientific survey) if people made their calls, got stuff by fax, or made copies while parked or if they would pull over and do it.

But there is something totally unnerving about being on the expressway, doing 75 mph just to keep up with traffic, and looking over to the fast lane to see some jerk in a Mercedes or BMW talking on the phone. You just know they're talking to their broker, or returning a call to people who are returning their call and who are probably whizzing by on the opposite side of the expressway right now, also scaring the people in that middle lane.

Okay, okay, not *everyone* is a jerk. Some people need to be able to keep in touch with the office, or their families, or other people. Physicians, for instance. Den mothers. Our friend Larry Graham.

Thanks to cellular technology, there are phones on airplanes, on trains, in cars. There's probably a phone booth at the bottom of the Grand Canyon. Maybe what really bothers me is that there is no place now where you can officially get away from the phone.

Secret #249 Your business is as good as your word.

If you have promised someone you'll deliver a job or part of a job by a certain date, do it.

Even if you get a terrible cold, do it.

Even if you miss a night of sleep, do it.

Even if you don't need the work or the money, do it.

Even though you may hate what you're doing, do it.

Even if you feel as though you're not the best person for the job, do it.

Even if you had a big fight with your lover and you are not thinking straight, do it.

Even if you've in over your head, do it.

Even if you know that you'll never do anything for this client again, do it.

Even if it costs you more money than what you'll get paid because you have to hire someone else to finish it for you, do it.

The only legitimate ways to get out of this with your sense of honor intact would be that you either: (a) die, or (b) discover you're involved in something illegal and you might get sent to jail if you do whatever it is the client wants you to do.

Not coming through when you say you will might not have any effect at all, or it might contribute to the climate that creates another recession. You have no idea how many other people may be depending on you to come through with your piece of the puzzle, on time.

Environmental and
Recycling Information

Secret #250 Death to meetings!

The Rosetta stone, commonly thought of as the key to the deciphering of Egyptian hieroglyphics, is actually a record of all the notes taken at all the meetings held on the earth between the beginning of time and approximately A.D. 1750; there were maybe 27 in all.

From Italy the world received the Renaissance; from France came wine and cheese parties; Russia sold us on how great we could look in huge overcoats. But the major contribution that America made to history was bringing about meetings.

During America's pioneer years, regular meetings started to come into vogue. Guys at those early meetings would gather around the lead guy's wagon, snorting and spitting a lot, betting each other how fur they could git by Saturday. Meanwhile, support personnel were cooking, washing up, feeding babies and livestock, gathering up kindling and berries, repairing wagons and boots, sewing, and sweeping small things such as entire moose families out of the wagon.

Over the following century, the concept of requiring staff members to attend long, boring meetings for business reasons was heavily promoted by American industry as a way to take up valuable time during work days, forcing conscientious people to come in on weekends to finish their work. But people began to realize that they needed regular two-day weekends so they could catch up with life and get to know those large, looming strangers in the kitchen or family room called "children."

I just have one question for you big bully bosses out there: other than getting coffee, *what is the purpose of meetings?*

First of all, the lighting is usually that overhead bluish corporate coffin look, enhancing every line in your otherwise young face. Second, everybody acts differently in meetings, all formal and stiff, when you know for a fact that the guy across from you wrapped a towel around his head last night and sang "Baby, It's You" in the bar next door, then burped sloppily 12 times in a row.

Meetings cost time and money. They can really break up a day and cause you to get hopelessly behind in everything. This is because no one, with the possible exception of Douglas Brackman on "L.A. Law," knows how to conduct a meeting and keep it moving.

Plus, for the owner of a small business, meetings are environmentally wasteful. Why use gas and pollute the air to drive to a meeting that isn't necessary?

There are, however, going to be times that you really need to talk with people about projects, deadlines, prices, and other elements critical to your small business. So here are a few suggestions for ways to eliminate meetings from your business (and personal) life, and still get all the facts you need to do your work efficiently:

1. Pick up the telephone. Long thought of as merely a device with which to order pizza, this remarkable invention doubles as a two-way information exchange for businesses. Some telephones can even do conference or multi-line calls, an idea picked up from some of our lovely government agencies, with the major difference being that everyone knows who is listening in on a conference call.

2. Send a letter/proposal/memo by mail.

3. Or send the stupid thing by fax.

4. Get together (don't say "meet") for lunch. This is for those wheeler-dealers who think foreplay is something you do in business. You know who they are— they want to negotiate everything, deal you down, cut you in, play the game. Why are you even working with this type of person? Make them pick up the tab.

If you just can't avoid it, take charge of it. Have your agenda written out. Meet the people you have to meet, say the things you have to say, and clear out.

Secret #251 How to lose one pound per week and help save the environment.

You're the first to know this—running your own business is actually the diet plan of the nineties. If you follow these suggestions, you're going to lose weight and you're not going to pollute the air, unless you forget to take a shower for five days in a row.

Walk or ride your bike to the bank.

You can still laugh all the way. Who needs to drive if your bank is close by?

SAFETY TIP (which has nothing to do with environmental concerns): Wear old sloppy clothes with big inside pockets. Don't carry a purse or visible envelope. I've made $25,000 check deposits while looking like a street person. Robbers tend to look for people who look as though they have money. And don't always go at the same time or on the same day. Sure tip-off for muggers.

Walk to the nearest mailbox, or ride your bike.

Why make your mail carrier do all the work? It's bad enough that he or she has to drag tons of mail to your home or office every day. By the way, don't forget to give this nearly free courier service a nice bonus at Christmas time.

Walk or ride your bike to do errands.

Going to the stationery supply store? Get big baskets for your bike, or carry a pack on your back. Or better yet, place your larger orders by phone to be delivered, and just ride your bike around for an hour.

If you can get in a walk or ride just about every day, you'll relieve some of the stress of constant working, and you'll feel fabulous—not to mention how great you'll look.

If you have to go to meetings, why not ride your bike?

Take it into the meeting with you, or at least make sure everyone sees you wheeling it in and leaving it in the lobby. They already know that you are a free spirit and that you do things like this. It's not advisable to wear heels while riding your bike, however.

Secret #252 Arc on over for a cup of coffee sometime.

Okay, so you get your computer hooked up, and you attach your printer to the computer, and the modem to the computer, and you plug in the copier, the fax machine, maybe the coffee maker, the little microwave, a few lamps, your electric pencil sharpener, a portable heater and maybe a tiny fridge. Your home office is perfect.

And you drag everybody into your perfect little office and turn on all the lights and magic at once—

—Snap! Crackle! Pop!

You have just blown every fuse in the house.

If you work out of a home which was built before the time when Ike carried his own golf clubs, or possibly before the invention of golf clubs, you may have to do some serious rewiring.

At least hire an electrician to test each outlet and replace poor wiring where necessary, before you plug in any equipment.

You sort of become a nuclear power plant advocate when you get this dependent on electricity, but you can still try to keep a lid on usage and costs by not leaving equipment such as copiers on continuously, and by making sure that your power system is as efficient as it can be.

Secret #253 Stop that junk mail.

This is heavy duty stuff. These figures are truly awful:

1. Americans receive about *four million tons* of junk mail each year. That is approximately a lot of junk mail per household.

2. About half of that is never opened. It just gets pitched.

3. This junk directly wastes the earth's resources, pollutes the water, and piles up higher on the trash heaps.

4. Only you can stop it from coming. You don't think the direct mail people are going to take action here, do you?

5. Write to this place below and ask them to remove your personal and company names and addresses from large mailing list companies and to please never sell or rent your name to any other organization. They'll do this free of charge. It takes three to four months because they update the list quarterly, so if you just miss the cutoff, they won't get it until the next quarter.

> Direct Marketing Association
> Mail Preference Service
> 11 West 42nd St.
> P.O. Box 3861
> New York, NY 10163-3861

If you hate to write letters like this, I've made it easy for you. Use the following form.

Date: _____

TO: Direct Marketing Association
     Mail Preference Service
     11 West 42nd St.
     P.O. Box 3861
     New York, NY 10163-3861

To whom it may concern:

Please remove the following names and addresses from all mailing lists that you possibly can, and do not rent or sell these names to any other organizations in the future:

_____

_____

_____

_____

_____

_____

Thank you very much.

                       Sincerely,

                       (Your name here)

Secret #254 Turn garbage into money.

Good news, America—you can make money by recycling paper. All kinds of companies, large and small, are raking in cash by tossing their waste paper into recycling cans and bins instead of the trash cans.

Kitzing Inc., a trade-show marketing firm in Chicago, turned in over half a ton of paper that employees had saved over a three-month period, and they received a check for $46 from a local recycling company.

Okay, so maybe it's not enough money to retire on, but you could probably pay for pizzas for the office gang.

Marriott Corporation in Bethesda, MD, turns in 18 tons of waste paper per month to U.S. Recycling of Hagerstown, MD, a recycling company that processes and sells the recycled paper to Fort Howard Paper Company, which turns around and sells it back to Marriott for use in its restaurants and hotels. Talk about your continuous loop.

The key to any of these recycling programs is doing it yourself, and getting any of the people who work with you to do it. Recycling one ton of paper saves 7,000 gallons of water, enough to keep your average busy household's showers and washing machines supplied with water for a month. I'm not even going to mention that every ton of paper not sent to a landfill saves three cubic yards of landfill space, or that each recovered ton of paper can conserve the energy equivalent of 384 gallons of oil.

(I promised my editor I would not preach.)

Secret #255 Look good while you do it.

Saving paper and other recyclable stuff can be a drag storage-wise, as you probably know from your efforts at home. (If you are one of the very few people left who does not recycle things like newspapers, cans, and glass at home, I'm not speaking to you until you start.)

You can use bags, or big old cardboard boxes, or you can order bright, pretty containers from these places:

> Better Environment Inc.
> 480 Clinton Ave.
> Albany, NY 12206

Manufactures the Trashcycler, a unit with two containers and a shelf for newspapers.

> Environment in Mind
> P.O. Box 233
> Rifton, NY 12471

They sell a newspaper stacker with a built-in tying and cutting system.

> Hold Everything
> Mail Order Department
> P.O. Box 7807
> San Francisco, CA 94120-7807
> 1-800/421-2264

Everything you can imagine to help you recycle with style and class. Stand-up bins, portable carts that roll to curbside, stackable bins, shopping carts and bags, and the niftiest-looking trash cans and receptacles. Call the toll-free number for a catalog.

> Mid-Atlantic Waste Systems
> P.O. Box 1959
> Easton, MD 21601

Offers a Mobile Tripod, which is a 45-gallon container with three compartments that lift out, and a mobile aluminum cart that stacks plastic bins vertically

> Paperboy Products
> 601 Glenway St.
> Madison, WI 53711

Sells the Original Paperboy, a cardboard box for stacking newspapers with side slats for efficient bundling.

> Rubbermaid Inc.
> 1147 Akron Rd.
> Wooster, OH 44691

Sells a variety of stackable recycling boxes through mail order or through major department stores everywhere.

> Windsor Barrel Works
> P.O. Box 47
> Kempton, PA 19529

Offers lots of types of receptacles for office recycling.

Secret #256 More ways to sew a silk ear from a sow's purse (well, it's cruel to use her ear).

Here's a really fantastic way to get rich off this recycling paper gig—start a recycle center yourself. If you are interested in doing this, contact the people at the Solid Waste Association of North America (SWANA):

> SWANA
> P.O. Box 7219
> Silver Spring, MD 20910
> Phone: 301/585-2898

They can send you information about how to start a recycling center, and they have a program you can participate in to learn how to start it up and keep it going.

Another place to write to about this is:

> Recycle Management Co.
> P.O. Box 1607
> Lake Havasu City, AZ 86403
> Phone: 602/453-1481

For a small fee, they will send you a publication called *How to Start and Operate a Recycling Business*.

Secret #257 The ashtrays in the Rolls are filled, so let's send it to the dump.

If you invested in a laser printer for your computer, then you will need to replace the cartridge every now and then. Tossing used laser printer cartridges into the trash is not only throwing money away, it's also environmentally wasteful and potentially toxic. Plus nobody cool does this.

Thousands of businesses, including many agencies of the federal government, are now recycling laser cartridges instead of pitching them and buying new ones. In fact, people who own laser cartridge recycling businesses are really cleaning up.

For about half the cost of buying a new one, and often within two or three days, a reliable cartridge recycling lab will take apart and clean your used cartridge, replace old parts, and refill the toner bin. Any quality reconditioner will use a superior toner and will replace any of the components that have worn out. If this isn't done properly, or if only the toner gets replaced, you can end up with an inferior cartridge that prints poorly, and it might leak, which is really nice for the inside of your valuable laser printer.

One national company that does this service well is Cartridge Technology Network Inc., a family-run business that started with the lucrative D.C. market and expanded the service to 20 cities across the country. The company's research figures show that recycled cartridges comprised 10% of the cartridge business in 1992.

Automated Office Products, a Lanham, Maryland-based company, has an unusual twist on their cartridge reconditioning business. For each cartridge that you give to them instead of tossing in the trash, they will make a $5.00 donation in your company's name to a non profit organization such as Chesapeake Bay Foundation or United Way, which your company can claim as a valid income tax deduction. Single used cartridges can be mailed with self-addressed, postage-paid labels provided by Automated Office Products. For more information, call the company at 301/731-4000 or 1-800/673-8553.

P.S. If you own a DeskJet printer that uses disposable ink cartridges, you can refill these cartridges yourself with a JetFill, which is this fat syringe-like thing. When you use the injector, it looks like you're giving your DeskJet printer a huge shot. You can order a JetFill from:

JetFill America
2021 Guadalupe, Suite 8A
Austin, TX 78705
Phone: 1-800/749-2993; 512/469-5647

Secret #258 Facts on the fax paper.

As great as the fax machine is, it's a turkey, paper-wise speaking. Ordinary fax paper is not biodegradable, and it's not recyclable.

There are a few things an environmentally conscious business person can do about the fax machine:

1. Start the only type of business left for which you don't need a fax machine, which would obviously be selling tofu hot dogs at bungee jumping events;

2. Invest a fortune to buy a laser fax, which uses plain, recyclable paper, hooks into your computer network, is ultra high speed, and comes equipped with more memory than your kid sister who saw what you and your date did after the prom;

3. Try recycled paper in your fax. You can order it in standard roll lengths from places such as Earth Care Paper Inc., which sells all types of beautiful recycled paper products. Their fax paper contains 10% post-consumer waste content, and they honestly admit in their catalog that no thermal fax paper is yet recyclable. For a free copy of their catalog, which was printed on recycled paper using soy inks and which shows all types of paper products for your office and home, as well as describes their views about recycling, write:

Earth Care Paper Inc.
P.O. Box 7070
Madison, WI 53707
Phone: 608/277-2900.

HOT TIP: If you can't do anything else, at least skip the cover sheets. They're so unnecessary. If you send five fax pages a day, you'll save six rolls of paper a year by eliminating the cover sheets. Just write to whom you are sending the fax message at the top of the page and the number of pages that are coming. Or use a fax transmission sticker.

FINAL HOT TIP: The *Recycled Products Guide* is a directory that lists 57 categories of recycled paper products. You can send for it by calling 1-800/267-0707.

P.S.

Secret #259   Yes, that is a tidal wave, and yes, you are going to get wet.

Slowly, inevitably, the trend is toward more home-centered businesses of all types and sizes. For many of us, after years of officially going out to work, change is beginning to occur. We are standing at the edge of it, about to be engulfed by it.

In his marvelous, futuristic book, *The Third Wave,* published in 1980, Alvin Toffler describes the First Wave as being the agricultural revolution which swept over the entire planet, changing the migratory hunting and foraging habits of our ancestors into an entirely new way of life.

The Second Wave occurred when the Industrial Revolution spread across most of the earth, bringing with it the plants, steel mills, pink Cadillacs, factories, Legos, railroads, jets, hot rollers, and other behemoths of our industrialized civilization.

The Third Wave is what is happening all around us right now, what Toffler envisioned as a super-industrial society, a global crisscrossing of communications and data, what others have called the Age of Information, the Electronic Era, the Global Village, a scientific-technological revolution. It is the time of the electronic cottage, or the paperless office.

If the world was not ready for this in 1980, it's here now.

We are living in the brightest, boldest, most fascinating days in all of recorded history. There are far more options open to each of us. There has never been a better time to start your own information-oriented service business, and for many people, there's no better place to start it than right at home.

Working at home is going to help more people manage their time and lives better, and it holds the possibility of helping to solve more of our country's problems than anyone can imagine. It may not be for everyone, but I believe that working at home is one of the most wonderful options to come along since the cacao bean was discovered and people thought that this chocolate-tasting thing might have some possibilities.

Secret #260 One of the secrets of life.

When you ask 100 people what would make them happy, 99 are going to say that they want to get rich quickly, with little effort.

This only happens when you win the lottery, which can come with its own unique set of problems, I understand.

(If it makes you feel any better, the guy next door to a couple of my best friends in Pennsylvania won $5 million in that state's lottery. From what I've heard, he's still as miserable, lonely, mean-spirited, and sexually frustrated as he was before he became an overnight multimillionaire.)

You don't start your own business so you can get rich by doing nothing. You start your own business because you want to achieve independence, because you want more flexibility in your life, because you genuinely love doing what you do, or because you're completely zonkers.

Getting rich is an offshoot that may happen, but generally it doesn't, at least not that I've read or heard about from all the people I've known and talked to about this.

However, it took me a decade to accept that we weren't going to become independently wealthy overnight from our business. It would be nice if everyone could learn from my experience, but that's not how life is. So I simply wish you good times, and the best of luck as you run your small business. Know that at least one person out here is rooting for you to make it.

Note to you, the reader:

Thank you for taking the time to read my book. I hope it was helpful and somewhat entertaining.

If you would care to write and let me know how you're doing in your business, or if you would like to share any of your hard-earned, hard-learned secrets with me, send a letter or card to me in care of:

Avon Books
Attention: Publicity Department
(The address should be in the front of this book).

I promise I'll write you back, unless you sound wiggy or something.

Who knows? You may even see your secret or tip in my next book.

Thanks again. See you around the old watering hole.